HEALTHY GOURMET
CHEESECAKES

SIMPLE RECIPES FOR SENSATIONAL CHEESECAKES

KRIS ERICKSON

Avery Publishing Group
Garden City Park, New York

Cover Designer: William Gonzalez and Rudy Shur
Cover Photo Credit: ENVISION © Amy Reichman
Text Illustrator: John Wincek
Interior Color Photographs: Victor Giordano
Photo Food Stylist: BC Giordano
Typesetter: Elaine V. McCaw
In-House Editor: Marie Caratozzolo
Printer: Paragon Press, Honesdale, PA

Avery Publishing Group
120 Old Broadway
Garden City Park, NY 11040
1-800-548-5757

Cataloging-in-Publication Data

Erickson, Kris.
  Healthy gourmet cheesecakes : simple recipes for sensational
cheesecakes / by Kris Erickson.
    p.   cm.
  Includes index.
  ISBN 0–89529–783–3
  1. Cheesecake (Cookery).   2. Low-fat diet—Recipes.   I. Title.
TX773.E732   1998
641.8′653—dc21   97–31232
                                                          CIP

Copyright © 1998 by Kris Erickson

Printed in the United States of America

10 9 8 7 6 5 4 3 2 1

Contents

Dedicated to my husband, Michael.

Acknowledgments

Feeding ourselves in a responsible way has become increasingly important. The more we realize food's critical role in maintaining good health, the more we must think about what we eat.

Although I believe in eating healthy, I also believe in enjoying what I eat. Cutting fat and calories is important, but so is taste. You might say that I have cooking in my blood. It was one of the first skills I learned. When I was just five years old, I can remember my Mom interrupting her gossip session with our next-door neighbor to call over the fence, "Kris! Put the chicken and potatoes in the oven and start the broccoli."

Of course, fine cooking involves much more than the ability to bake chicken and potatoes. I learned many other cooking skills while growing up. And I've had many fine teachers. The first was my grandmother, Anna Cafera, who showed me how to make three-cheese ravioli from scratch. My Uncle Gerald Cafera introduced me to halvah (a sesame candy). He contributed to my appreciation of food by teaching me the difference between vichyssoise and plain potato soup. My friend and "adopted" mother, Jan Bennett, taught me how to make award-winning bread. She also gave me free reign in her kitchen to experiment while I was away from home during my college years. These valuable teachers taught me the importance of quality; of tasting everything and noticing subtle differences.

Other friends who have been an inspiration through their patience and willingness to try every cheesecake I created are Karen Campbell, Hollis Campbell, Diane Zimmerman, Bill Zimmerman, and Jennifer Davis.

I would like to thank my husband, Michael, for running to the supermarket at midnight for cream cheese and gelatin, and for filling in around the house so I could complete this cookbook.

I would also like to thank Victor Giordano for the wonderful photos and Jon Wincek for the creative drawings found throughout the book. And a final thank you to Rudy Shur, Joanne Abrams, and Marie Caratozzolo at Avery Publishing Group, who, through their excellent suggestions and guidance, helped shape my recipes into this lovely book.

Introduction

What comes to mind when you think of cheesecake? I picture thick wedges of rich, dense, creamy cake, topped with just the right garnish. Satisfyingly delicious, yes. But what about all that fat?

Being the passionate cheesecake addict that I am, I wasn't about to give up my favorite dessert without a fight. Determined, I set out to develop delicious, fat-free and low-fat gourmet cheesecake recipes, complete with crusts. Considering my high standards, however, I wondered if such a mission was even possible.

After gathering an assortment of my favorite "fat-filled" cheesecake recipes, I began making ingredient adjustments. I tested and retested. I was pleased to discover the ready availability of low-fat and fat-free counterparts of such high-fat items as cream cheese and sour cream—ingredients necessary for luscious cheesecakes. It was these very products that allowed me to meet with success in developing recipes for the fat-free restaurant-quality cheesecake I was searching for.

Eventually I developed four sensational basic recipes, which serve as the foundations for a myriad of taste-tempting cheesecake varieties. These basic recipes include a cream cheese-based cake, another made with tofu, one made with ricotta cheese, and finally, a lactose-free variety. Each flavorful cheesecake creation in this book begins with one of these four recipes as its base, but feel free to choose any of the basic recipes as the foundation for any cake you select.

Once I had established these basic recipes, it was time to experiment further. I began by adding standard fruit flavors to the batter, which turned out wonderfully. Soon, in addition to the basic strawberry, cherry, and blueberry cheesecakes, I found myself experimenting with more unusual flavors. This resulted in such cheesecakes as Piña Colada, Honey Tangerine, and Raspberry Royale.

Encouraged with the success of my fruit-flavored cakes, I turned my attention to chocolate—my passion. I created cheesecakes made with dark chocolate, milk chocolate, white chocolate, double chocolate, chocolate chips, and chocolate mocha—all delicious and all chocolaty enough to satisfy the cravings of the most demanding chocoholic.

But my cheesecake adventures didn't end there. I found that I had become a woman obsessed with creating cheesecakes with new and exciting tastes. From flavorful liqueurs, extracts, and essences, I developed such one-of-a kind cheesecakes as Creamy Kahlua, Rose Petal, and Butterscotch Sundae. After exhausting an extensive repertoire of flavors, I began combining two and even three flavors to make sensational layered cheesecakes. Absolutely beautiful and undeniably delicious.

And just when I thought I had created my last cheesecake flavor, I realized I had forgotten about no-bake cakes. Once again, I developed four basic recipes for no-bake cheesecakes, from which sprang a multitude of flavorful variations.

And now I am sharing my recipes for cheesecake success with you. You will find my cheesecakes easy to make and practically foolproof. In fact, they are so simple, you may find it hard to stop making them. Follow the recipes as written or use them as springboards to create your own flavorful masterpieces. Whatever you choose, I only hope that you derive as much satisfaction and pleasure from making and serving these cakes as I have.

1.
Creating Perfect Cheesecakes

Creating rich and creamy fat-free cheesecakes is simpler than you may think. Of course, during my search for the perfect basic recipe, I must admit that it took a lot of experimenting. I tried the cheesecakes offered by every restaurant, bakery, friend, and relative that I knew. During my research, I gathered as many cheesecake recipes that I could get my hands on and made each and every one. I spent month after month testing, adjusting, then testing some more. The cheesecake I was after had to have both great taste and rich, creamy texture.

It wasn't easy, but eventually I developed what I believe to be the perfect fat-free cheesecake and its variations. Now, I'd like to share my recipe secrets with you, so that you, too, can create perfect cheesecakes every time.

INGREDIENTS

During my search for the perfect cheesecake, I discovered the best basic cheesecake batter is made with cream cheese, sour cream, eggs, cream, butter, sugar, lemon juice, and vanilla extract. Once I made this discovery, I had to figure out how to replace the full-fat ingredients with fat-free ones.

As there are a number of excellent brands of fat-free cream cheese and sour cream on the market today, using them instead of their full-fat counterparts was easy. I also found egg substitute to be a fine replacement for whole eggs. As lemon juice and vanilla extract add no calories (in the small amounts used) and no fat, I was able to keep them in my recipes.

Replacing the butter was a little trickier. I tried a number of butter-flavored powders, but they didn't add enough flavor and did nothing for the texture. Low-fat margarines worked well enough, but I wanted fat-free. A number of fat-free margarines worked well, and I found Promise Ultra to be the best. It adds just enough flavor and has only 5 calories per tablespoon.

The cream was a bit of a puzzle, too. At first, I tried replacing it with evaporated milk, which tastes similar to cream in baked goods and has only half the calories. But again, it was not fat-free. One day, I was mixing up some nonfat dry milk, when I noticed that adding a small amount of water to the powder resulted in a thick, creamy liquid. I tried it in my next cheesecake attempt, and found that it added just the right fullness and creaminess to give the cake a rich dimension.

Granulated cane sugar is one ingredient I can live with, and it is called for in the majority of my recipes. Many people, however, may prefer other sweeteners. For this reason, I have provided the following sugar exchange information for your convenience. Feel free to use the sweetener of your choice in any recipe.

¾ cup granulated cane sugar =	½ cup honey
	½ cup fruit concentrate
	⅔ cup fructose
	¾ cup granulated brown sugar
	3 tablespoons sugar substitute
	(Equal, NutraSweet, etc.)

After much kitchen-testing, I finally succeeded in developing what I believe to be the perfect Basic Fat-Free Cheesecake (page 38). I was then able to take this basic recipe and create a wealth of variations from it. And you can, too.

I also went on to develop a Basic Tofu Cheesecake (page 40). Tofu adds a little fat, but its nutritional richness cannot be denied. It is high in protein and calcium, and contains all eight essential amino acids. What's more, tofu contains no cholesterol. There is also a Basic Fat-Free Ricotta Cheesecake (page 42) and a low-fat Basic Lactose-Free Cheesecake (page 44). You can use any of these four basic recipes as the basis for any cheesecake in this book.

PROPER EQUIPMENT

I don't like to buy cooking equipment that I rarely use, so I was careful to develop my cheesecake recipes using just a few basic pieces of equipment—no unique baking pans or gourmet utensils. The only items you will need to make my healthy gourmet cheesecakes are a mixing bowl, a rubber spatula, and an electric mixer or food processor. I use either a standard 6-inch or 9-inch springform pan, or a cupcake tin to bake the cakes, and an 8-inch pie pan for the no-bake cheesecakes.

Most springform pans are moderately priced at under ten dollars. The best thing is that you can use them to bake other foods. In addition to cheesecakes, I use them for casseroles, pies, pizzas, and vegetable dishes.

Although it isn't necessary, I prefer using a pastry bag with a star or rosette tip to pipe the whipped topping onto my finished cheesecakes. This nominal purchase will help make your finished creation very elegant.

IMPORTANT BAKING TIPS

Once the batter is prepared, spoon it over the crust in a springform pan and smooth it evenly with a rubber spatula. Place the pan on the center oven rack. This oven placement is very important. If the cheesecake is placed too high, the top will burn and turn an unappealing brown. If it sits too low, the cake won't cook fast enough and the center will be soft. You may find that even when the pan is placed in the center of the oven, the top may begin to brown too quickly. If this happens, simply cover the top loosely with aluminum foil.

You can test the cake for doneness by lightly tapping on the side of the pan. If the center of the pan shakes like a waterbed mattress, you can be sure the cake isn't done. Continue testing for doneness every 5 minutes until the center of the cheesecake is firm to the touch.

Remove the cheesecake from the oven and place it on a wire rack until it is completely cool (about 2 hours). Once cool, place the cake in the refrigerator for at least 2 hours. The chilled cake will come out of the pan easily. Loosen the cake from the sides of the pan with a knife or metal spatula before removing it.

ABOUT THE RECIPES IN THIS BOOK

Recipe directions in this book are given for 6-inch and 9-inch cheesecakes. Nutritional analysis is based on 4-ounce servings. The 6-inch cheesecake yields eight servings, while the 9-inch cake yields sixteen. To make a dozen cupcakes, follow the instructions for the 6-inch cake. For two dozen, follow the instructions for the 9-inch cake.

The no-bake cheesecakes found in Chapters 9 and 10 are not made in springform pans. Rather, they are prepared in 8-inch pie plates. Instructions are given for one and two pies.

With the exception of the no-bake cheesecakes, all of the cakes are garnished with a little low-fat whipped topping and a variety of other ingredients such as grated orange and lemon zest, cocoa powder, and assorted berries. But do know that these garnishes, which generally include less that 1 gram of fat per serving, are optional.

Well, that's it! You're ready to start. Let's make cheesecake!

2.

The Perfect Crust

Much of the fat in a standard cheesecake is often hidden in the crust. I have created the following delicious low-fat and fat-free basic crusts for my cheesecakes. Each one takes only minutes to prepare and yields 1⅓ cups of crumbs. This amount is enough to make a thick crust for a standard 6-inch cheesecake, and crusts for a dozen cupcake-sized servings. For a 9-inch cheesecake, simply double the recipe.

When preparing the dough, which is stiff, I prefer using the dough hooks on my electric mixer, but you can use regular beaters as well. And all of the crumbs can be used in their dry form without adding the melted margarine. Simply press the dry crumbs into the bottom of the pan before adding the cheesecake filling.

I have suggested certain crusts for each of my cheesecake recipes, but feel free to make your own choices. Finally, you can double or triple any of the crust recipes and freeze the extra crumbs for up to a month.

Graham Cracker Crust

INGREDIENT	FOR 6-INCH CRUST	FOR 9-INCH CRUST
All-purpose flour	⅔ cups	1⅓ cups
Whole wheat flour	¼ cup	½ cup
Dark brown sugar, packed	3 tablespoons	6 tablespoons
Salt	⅛ teaspoon	¼ teaspoon
Honey	1½ tablespoons	3 tablespoons
Fat-free margarine, softened	1 tablespoon	2 tablespoons
Vanilla	½ teaspoon	1 teaspoon
Water	1½ tablespoons	3 tablespoons
Fat-free margarine, melted	2 tablespoons	¼ cup

Serves	8	16
Calories per serving	85	85
Fat per serving	0 gram	0 gram

With few calories and absolutely no fat, this tasty graham cracker crust is the perfect base for any cheesecake.

---

1. Preheat the oven to 325°F. Spray a cookie sheet with nonstick cooking spray and set aside.

2. Combine the flours, brown sugar, and salt in an electric mixing bowl. Add the honey, softened margarine, and vanilla, and mix until combined. Add just enough water to make the dough hold together. The dough will be stiff.

3. Pat or roll out the dough on the cookie sheet in a thin, even "cookie."

4. Place in the oven and bake about 15 minutes until evenly browned.

5. Allow the cookie to cool, then break it into a blender or food processor and finely grind.

6. Place the crumbs in a small bowl, add the melted margarine, and mix together.

7. Press the moistened crumbs on the bottom and partially up the sides of a greased springform pan. Add the cheesecake filling and bake as directed in the individual recipe.

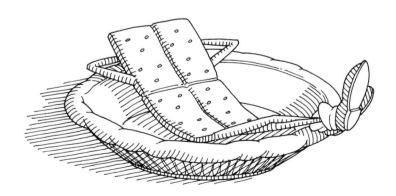

Chocolate Graham Cracker Crust

INGREDIENT	FOR 6-INCH CRUST	FOR 9-INCH CRUST
All-purpose flour	⅔ cups	1⅓ cups
Whole wheat flour	¼ cup	½ cup
European-style cocoa	2 tablespoons	¼ cup
Dark brown sugar, packed	3 tablespoons	6 tablespoons
Salt	⅛ teaspoon	¼ teaspoon
Honey	1½ tablespoons	3 tablespoons
Fat-free margarine, softened	1 tablespoon	2 tablespoons
Vanilla	½ teaspoon	1 teaspoon
Water	1½ tablespoons	3 tablespoons
Fat-free margarine, melted	2 tablespoons	¼ cup

Serves	8	16
Calories per serving	91 (5 from fat)	91 (5 from fat)
Fat per serving	0.6 gram	0.6 gram

This sensational chocolate-flavored crust has only about a half gram of fat per serving.

---

1. Preheat the oven to 325°F. Spray a cookie sheet with nonstick cooking spray and set aside.

2. Combine the flours, cocoa, brown sugar, and salt in an electric mixing bowl. Add the honey, softened margarine, and vanilla, and mix until combined. Add just enough water to make the dough hold together. The dough will be stiff.

3. Pat or roll out the dough on the cookie sheet in a thin, even "cookie."

4. Place in the oven and bake about 15 minutes until evenly browned.

5. Allow the cookie to cool, then break it into a blender or food processor and finely grind.

6. Place the crumbs in a small bowl, add the melted margarine, and mix together.

7. Press the moistened crumbs on the bottom and partially up the sides of a greased springform pan. Add the cheesecake filling and bake as directed in the individual recipe.

Zesty Orange Graham Cracker Crust

INGREDIENT	FOR 6-INCH CRUST	FOR 9-INCH CRUST
All-purpose flour	⅔ cups	1⅓ cups
Whole wheat flour	¼ cup	½ cup
Dark brown sugar, packed	3 tablespoons	6 tablespoons
Salt	⅛ teaspoon	¼ teaspoon
Honey	1½ tablespoons	3 tablespoons
Fat-free margarine, softened	1 tablespoon	2 tablespoons
Vanilla	½ teaspoon	1 teaspoon
Orange juice	1½ tablespoons	3 tablespoons
Orange zest	1 teaspoon	2 teaspoons
Fat-free margarine, melted	2 tablespoons	¼ cup

Serves	8	16
Calories per serving	85	85
Fat per serving	0 gram	0 gram

This fat-free crust is especially nice with cheesecakes such as Honey Tangerine (page 64), and Orange Creamsicle (page 186).

---

1. Preheat the oven to 325°F. Spray a cookie sheet with nonstick cooking spray and set aside.

2. Combine the flours, brown sugar, and salt in an electric mixing bowl. Add the honey, softened margarine, and vanilla, and mix until combined. Add just enough orange juice to make the dough hold together. The dough will be stiff.

3. Pat or roll out the dough on the cookie sheet in a thin, even "cookie."

4. Place in the oven and bake about 15 minutes until evenly browned.

5. Allow the cookie to cool, then break it into a blender or food processor and finely grind.

6. Place the crumbs in a small bowl along with the orange zest, add the melted margarine, and mix together.

7. Press the moistened crumbs on the bottom and partially up the sides of a greased springform pan. Add the cheesecake filling and bake as directed in the individual recipe.

Lemony
Graham Cracker Crust

INGREDIENT	FOR 6-INCH CRUST	FOR 9-INCH CRUST
All-purpose flour	⅔ cups	1⅓ cups
Whole wheat flour	¼ cup	½ cup
Dark brown sugar, packed	3 tablespoons	6 tablespoons
Salt	⅛ teaspoon	¼ teaspoon
Honey	1½ tablespoons	3 tablespoons
Fat-free margarine, softened	1 tablespoon	2 tablespoons
Vanilla	½ teaspoon	1 teaspoon
Lemon juice	1½ tablespoons	3 tablespoons
Lemon zest	1 teaspoon	2 teaspoons
Fat-free margarine, melted	2 tablespoons	¼ cup

Serves	8	16
Calories per serving	85	85
Fat per serving	0 gram	0 gram

A hint of lemon makes this fat-free crust the perfect base for a number of fruit-flavored cheesecakes.

---

1. Preheat the oven to 325°F. Spray a cookie sheet with nonstick cooking spray and set aside.

2. Combine the flours, brown sugar, and salt in an electric mixing bowl. Add the honey, softened margarine, and vanilla, and mix until combined. Add just enough lemon juice to make the dough hold together. The dough will be stiff.

3. Pat or roll out the dough on the cookie sheet in a thin, even "cookie."

4. Place in the oven and bake about 15 minutes until evenly browned.

5. Allow the cookie to cool, then break it into a blender or food processor and finely grind.

6. Place the crumbs in a small bowl along with the lemon zest, add the melted margarine, and mix together.

7. Press the moistened crumbs on the bottom and partially up the sides of a greased springform pan. Add the cheesecake filling and bake as directed in the individual recipe.

Zesty Lime Graham Cracker Crust

INGREDIENT	FOR 6-INCH CRUST	FOR 9-INCH CRUST
All-purpose flour	⅔ cups	1⅓ cups
Whole wheat flour	¼ cup	½ cup
Dark brown sugar, packed	3 tablespoons	6 tablespoons
Salt	⅛ teaspoon	¼ teaspoon
Honey	1½ tablespoons	3 tablespoons
Fat-free margarine, softened	1 tablespoon	2 tablespoons
Vanilla	½ teaspoon	1 teaspoon
Lime juice	1½ tablespoons	3 tablespoons
Lime zest	1 teaspoon	2 teaspoons
Fat-free margarine, melted	2 tablespoons	¼ cup

Serves	8	16
Calories per serving	85	85
Fat per serving	0 gram	0 gram

Adding lime zest to this basic crust makes it the perfect choice for a number of cheesecakes. Be sure to try it with the No-Bake Lemon-Lime Cheesecake (page 308).

---

1. Preheat the oven to 325°F. Spray a cookie sheet with nonstick cooking spray and set aside.

2. Combine the flours, brown sugar, and salt in an electric mixing bowl. Add the honey, softened margarine, and vanilla, and mix until combined. Add just enough lime juice to make the dough hold together. The dough will be stiff.

3. Pat or roll out the dough on the cookie sheet in a thin, even "cookie."

4. Place in the oven and bake about 15 minutes until evenly browned.

5. Allow the cookie to cool, then break it into a blender or food processor and finely grind.

6. Place the crumbs in a small bowl along with the lime zest, add the melted margarine, and mix together.

7. Press the moistened crumbs on the bottom and partially up the sides of a greased springform pan. Add the cheesecake filling and bake as directed in the individual recipe.

Cinnamon Graham Cracker Crust

INGREDIENT	FOR 6-INCH CRUST	FOR 9-INCH CRUST
All-purpose flour	⅔ cups	1⅓ cups
Whole wheat flour	¼ cup	½ cup
Dark brown sugar, packed	3 tablespoons	6 tablespoons
Salt	⅛ teaspoon	¼ teaspoon
Honey	1½ tablespoons	3 tablespoons
Fat-free margarine, softened	1 tablespoon	2 tablespoons
Vanilla	½ teaspoon	1 teaspoon
Water	1½ tablespoons	3 tablespoons
Cinnamon	1 teaspoon	2 teaspoons
Fat-free margarine, melted	2 tablespoons	¼ cup

Serves	8	16
Calories per serving	85	85
Fat per serving	0 gram	0 gram

Just a hint of cinnamon gives this fat-free crust its unique taste. For an Oriental flair, substitute ground ginger for the cinnamon.

---

1. Preheat the oven to 325°F. Spray a cookie sheet with nonstick cooking spray and set aside.

2. Combine the flours, brown sugar, and salt in an electric mixing bowl. Add the honey, softened margarine, and vanilla, and mix until combined. Add just enough water to make the dough hold together. The dough will be stiff.

3. Pat or roll out the dough on the cookie sheet in a thin, even "cookie."

4. Place in the oven and bake about 15 minutes until evenly browned.

5. Allow the cookie to cool, then break it into a blender or food processor and finely grind.

6. Place the crumbs in a small bowl along with the cinnamon, add the melted margarine, and mix together.

7. Press the moistened crumbs on the bottom and partially up the sides of a greased springform pan. Add the cheesecake filling and bake as directed in the individual recipe.

Coconut
Graham Cracker Crust

INGREDIENT	FOR 6-INCH CRUST	FOR 9-INCH CRUST
All-purpose flour	⅔ cups	1⅓ cups
Whole wheat flour	¼ cup	½ cup
Dark brown sugar, packed	3 tablespoons	6 tablespoons
Salt	1/8 teaspoon	¼ teaspoon
Honey	1½ tablespoons	3 tablespoons
Fat-free margarine, softened	1 tablespoon	2 tablespoons
Vanilla	½ teaspoon	1 teaspoon
Water	1½ tablespoons	3 tablespoons
Coconut extract	1 teaspoon	2 teaspoons
Fat-free margarine, melted	2 tablespoons	¼ cup

Serves	8	16
Calories per serving	85	85
Fat per serving	0 gram	0 gram

Delicious and fat-free, this coconut-flavored crust has a decidedly tropical taste.

---

1. Preheat the oven to 325°F. Spray a cookie sheet with nonstick cooking spray and set aside.

2. Combine the flours, brown sugar, and salt in an electric mixing bowl. Add the honey, softened margarine, and vanilla, and mix until combined. Add just enough water to make the dough hold together. The dough will be stiff.

3. Pat or roll out the dough on the cookie sheet in a thin, even "cookie."

4. Place in the oven and bake about 15 minutes until evenly browned.

5. Allow the cookie to cool, then break it into a blender or food processor and finely grind.

6. Place the crumbs in a small bowl along with the coconut extract, add the melted margarine, and mix together.

7. Press the moistened crumbs on the bottom and partially up the sides of a greased springform pan. Add the cheesecake filling and bake as directed in the individual recipe.

Chewy Oat Crust

INGREDIENT	FOR 6-INCH CRUST	FOR 9-INCH CRUST
All-purpose flour	¼ cup	½ cup
Whole wheat flour	¼ cup	½ cup
Rolled oats	½ cup	1 cup
Dark brown sugar, packed	1 tablespoon	2 tablespoons
Salt	⅛ teaspoon	¼ teaspoon
Fat-free margarine, softened	1 tablespoon	2 tablespoons
Water	1½ tablespoons	3 tablespoons
Fat-free margarine, melted	2 tablespoons	¼ cup

Serves	8	16
Calories per serving	67 (4 from fat)	67 (4 from fat)
Fat per serving	0.5 gram	0.5 gram

This oat crust has a pleasant, slightly nutty flavor—with very little fat!

---

1. Preheat the oven to 350°F. Spray a cookie sheet with nonstick cooking spray and set aside.

2. Combine the flours, oats, brown sugar, and salt in an electric mixing bowl. Add the softened margarine and mix until combined. Add just enough water to make the dough hold together. The dough will be stiff.

3. Pat or roll out the dough on the cookie sheet in a thin, even "cookie."

4. Place in the oven and bake about 15 minutes until evenly browned.

5. Allow the cookie to cool, then break it into a blender or food processor and finely grind.

6. Place the crumbs in a small bowl, add the melted margarine, and mix together.

7. Press the moistened crumbs on the bottom and partially up the sides of a greased springform pan. Add the cheesecake filling and bake as directed in the individual recipe.

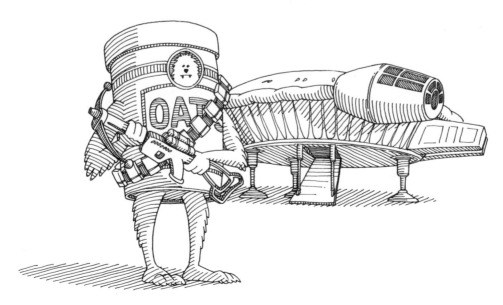

Zesty Orange Oat Crust

INGREDIENT	FOR 6-INCH CRUST	FOR 9-INCH CRUST
All-purpose flour	¼ cup	½ cup
Whole wheat flour	¼ cup	½ cup
Rolled oats	½ cup	1 cup
Dark brown sugar, packed	1 tablespoon	2 tablespoons
Salt	⅛ teaspoon	¼ teaspoon
Fat-free margarine, softened	1 tablespoon	2 tablespoons
Orange juice	1½ tablespoons	3 tablespoons
Grated orange zest	1 teaspoon	2 teaspoons
Fat-free margarine, melted	2 tablespoons	¼ cup

Serves	8	16
Calories per serving	67 (4 from fat)	67 (4 from fat)
Fat per serving	0.5 gram	0.5 gram

This very low-fat crust has just the right amount of orange zest to give it a wonderful flavor.

---

1. Preheat the oven to 350°F. Spray a cookie sheet with nonstick cooking spray and set aside.

2. Combine the flours, oats, brown sugar, and salt in an electric mixing bowl. Add the softened margarine and mix until combined. Add just enough orange juice to make the dough hold together. The dough will be stiff.

3. Pat or roll out the dough on the cookie sheet in a thin, even "cookie."

4. Place in the oven and bake about 15 minutes until evenly browned.

5. Allow the cookie to cool, then break it into a blender or food processor and finely grind.

6. Place the crumbs in a small bowl along with the orange zest, add the melted margarine, and mix together.

7. Press the moistened crumbs on the bottom and partially up the sides of a greased springform pan. Add the cheesecake filling and bake as directed in the individual recipe.

Lemony Oat Crust

INGREDIENT	FOR 6-INCH CRUST	FOR 9-INCH CRUST
All-purpose flour	¼ cup	½ cup
Whole wheat flour	¼ cup	½ cup
Rolled oats	½ cup	1 cup
Dark brown sugar, packed	1 tablespoon	2 tablespoons
Salt	⅛ teaspoon	¼ teaspoon
Fat-free margarine, softened	1 tablespoon	2 tablespoons
Lemon juice	1½ tablespoons	3 tablespoons
Grated lemon zest	1 teaspoon	2 teaspoons
Fat-free margarine, melted	2 tablespoons	¼ cup

Serves	8	16
Calories per serving	67 (4 from fat)	67 (4 from fat)
Fat per serving	0.5 gram	0.5 gram

Lemon zest gives this low-fat crust real zing.

---

1. Preheat the oven to 350°F. Spray a cookie sheet with nonstick cooking spray and set aside.

2. Combine the flours, oats, brown sugar, and salt in an electric mixing bowl. Add the softened margarine and mix until combined. Add just enough lemon juice to make the dough hold together. The dough will be stiff.

3. Pat or roll out the dough on the cookie sheet in a thin, even "cookie."

4. Place in the oven and bake about 15 minutes until evenly browned.

5. Allow the cookie to cool, then break it into a blender or food processor and finely grind.

6. Place the crumbs in a small bowl along with the lemon zest, add the melted margarine, and mix together.

7. Press the moistened crumbs on the bottom and partially up the sides of a greased springform pan. Add the cheesecake filling and bake as directed in the individual recipe.

Zesty Lime Oat Crust

INGREDIENT	FOR 6-INCH CRUST	FOR 9-INCH CRUST
All-purpose flour	¼ cup	½ cup
Whole wheat flour	¼ cup	½ cup
Rolled oats	½ cup	1 cup
Dark brown sugar, packed	1 tablespoon	2 tablespoons
Salt	⅛ teaspoon	¼ teaspoon
Fat-free margarine, softened	1 tablespoon	2 tablespoons
Lime juice	1½ tablespoons	3 tablespoons
Grated lime zest	1 teaspoon	2 teaspoons
Fat-free margarine, melted	2 tablespoons	¼ cup

Serves	8	16
Calories per serving	67 (4 from fat)	67 (4 from fat)
Fat per serving	0.5 gram	0.5 gram

Tasty and very low in fat, this crust is the perfect base for any of the lime-flavored cheesecakes in this book.

---

1. Preheat the oven to 350°F. Spray a cookie sheet with nonstick cooking spray and set aside.

2. Combine the flours, oats, brown sugar, and salt in an electric mixing bowl. Add the softened margarine and mix until combined. Add just enough lime juice to make the dough hold together. The dough will be stiff.

3. Pat or roll out the dough on the cookie sheet in a thin, even "cookie."

4. Place in the oven and bake about 15 minutes until evenly browned.

5. Allow the cookie to cool, then break it into a blender or food processor and finely grind.

6. Place the crumbs in a small bowl along with the lime zest, add the melted margarine, and mix together.

7. Press the moistened crumbs on the bottom and partially up the sides of a greased springform pan. Add the cheesecake filling and bake as directed in the individual recipe.

Cinnamon Oat Crust

INGREDIENT	FOR 6-INCH CRUST	FOR 9-INCH CRUST
All-purpose flour	¼ cup	½ cup
Whole wheat flour	¼ cup	½ cup
Rolled oats	½ cup	1 cup
Dark brown sugar, packed	1 tablespoon	2 tablespoons
Salt	⅛ teaspoon	¼ teaspoon
Fat-free margarine, softened	1 tablespoon	2 tablespoons
Water	1½ tablespoons	3 tablespoons
Cinnamon	1 teaspoon	2 teaspoons
Fat-free margarine, melted	2 tablespoons	¼ cup

Serves	8	16
Calories per serving	67 (4 from fat)	67 (4 from fat)
Fat per serving	0.5 gram	0.5 gram

Kids especially seem to love this crust. Be sure to try it with the Rum Raisin Cheesecake (page 138).

---

1. Preheat the oven to 350°F. Spray a cookie sheet with nonstick cooking spray and set aside.

2. Combine the flours, oats, brown sugar, and salt in an electric mixing bowl. Add the softened margarine and mix until combined. Add just enough water to make the dough hold together. The dough will be stiff.

3. Pat or roll out the dough on the cookie sheet in a thin, even "cookie."

4. Place in the oven and bake about 15 minutes until evenly browned.

5. Allow the cookie to cool, then break it into a blender or food processor and finely grind.

6. Place the crumbs in a small bowl along with the cinnamon, add the melted margarine, and mix together.

7. Press the moistened crumbs on the bottom and partially up the sides of a greased springform pan. Add the cheesecake filling and bake as directed in the individual recipe.

Coconut Oat Crust

INGREDIENT	FOR 6-INCH CRUST	FOR 9-INCH CRUST
All-purpose flour	¼ cup	½ cup
Whole wheat flour	¼ cup	½ cup
Rolled oats	½ cup	1 cup
Dark brown sugar, packed	1 tablespoon	2 tablespoons
Salt	⅛ teaspoon	¼ teaspoon
Fat-free margarine, softened	1 tablespoon	2 tablespoons
Water	1½ tablespoons	3 tablespoons
Coconut extract	1 teaspoon	2 teaspoons
Fat-free margarine, melted	2 tablespoons	¼ cup

Serves	8	16
Calories per serving	67 (4 from fat)	67 (4 from fat)
Fat per serving	0.5 gram	0.5 gram

Be sure to try this crust with the Piña Colada Cheesecake (page 52) and the Tutti-Frutti Cheesecake (page 128).

---

1. Preheat the oven to 350°F. Spray a cookie sheet with nonstick cooking spray and set aside.

2. Combine the flours, oats, brown sugar, and salt in an electric mixing bowl. Add the softened margarine and mix until combined. Add just enough water to make the dough hold together. The dough will be stiff.

3. Pat or roll out the dough on the cookie sheet in a thin, even "cookie."

4. Place in the oven and bake about 15 minutes until evenly browned.

5. Allow the cookie to cool, then break it into a blender or food processor and finely grind.

6. Place the crumbs in a small bowl along with the coconut extract, add the melted margarine, and mix together.

7. Press the moistened crumbs on the bottom and partially up the sides of a greased springform pan. Add the cheesecake filling and bake as directed in the individual recipe.

Flaky Phyllo Crust

INGREDIENT	FOR 6-INCH CRUST	FOR 9-INCH CRUST
Phyllo dough sheets	2, cut in half	4
Fat-free margarine, melted	¼ cup (½ stick)	½ cup (1 stick)

Serves	8	16
Calories per serving	45	45
Fat per serving	0 gram	0 gram

This simple crust of layered phyllo dough takes minutes to prepare. It is the perfect foundation for Baklava Cheesecake (page 148).

---

1. Stack the 2 sheets of phyllo for a 6-inch cake and cut them in half. For a 9-inch crust, simply stack the 4 sheets and cut them to fit the pan.

2. Spray the springform pan with cooking spray.

3. Place one of the phyllo sheets in the pan, pressing it gently to cover the bottom and sides. Brush with melted margarine and place a second sheet on top. Repeat procedure with the remaining two sheets. Fold any phyllo that is hanging over the sides and press it against the inside of the pan.

4. Pour the cheesecake batter gently into the pan and bake as directed.

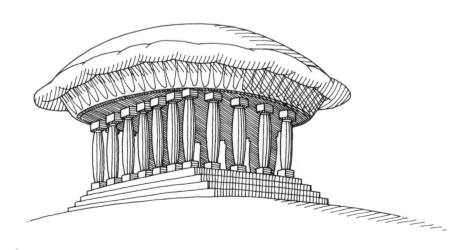

3.

Basic Cheesecakes

What better way to end a special meal than with a slice of fabulous cheesecake? The recipes presented in this chapter serve as the basics. They are the foundations for the vast array of cheesecake variations presented in this book.

For starters, you'll find the Basic Fat-Free Cheesecake, which is so rich and creamy, you'll be amazed that it's fat-free. There is also a tofu cheesecake, as well as a fat-free creation made with ricotta cheese. Lactose-intolerant? There's a fabulous lactose-free cheesecake just for you.

Although the majority of recipes in the remaining chapters are based on the Basic Fat-Free Cheesecake, feel free to use any of the recipes in this chapter as a luscious base for any cheesecake found in this book. And while sugar and honey are popularly used, know that you can substitute these ingredients with your own choice of sweeteners (a sugar substitution list is presented on page 4).

One thing I promise, no matter which of these cakes you try, you'll find each one to be sinfully rich, creamy, and delicious. They will have your guests asking for more.

Basic Fat-Free Cheesecake

INGREDIENT	FOR 6-INCH CAKE	FOR 9-INCH CAKE
Fat-free cream cheese, softened	3 8-ounce packages	6 8-ounce packages
Sugar	¾ cup	1½ cups
Fat-free egg substitute	4 ounces	8 ounces
Nonfat powdered milk	¼ cup mixed with 2 tablespoons water	½ cup mixed with ¼ cup water
Fat-free sour cream	¼ cup	½ cup
Fat-free margarine, melted	¼ cup	½ cup
All-purpose flour	¼ cup	½ cup
Fresh lemon juice	1 tablespoon	2 tablespoons
Vanilla extract	1 teaspoon	2 teaspoons
CRUST		
Graham Cracker (page 8)	single recipe	double recipe

Baking Time	45–60 minutes	1¼–1½ hours
Serves	8	16
Calories per serving	180	180
Fat per serving	0 gram	0 gram

This creamy cheesecake is so rich you will find it hard to believe that it has zero fat.

---

1. Preheat the oven to 350°F.

2. Gently pat the prepared crust mixture on the bottom and partially up the sides of a greased springform pan. Place in the freezer for 10 minutes.

3. Blend the cream cheese and sugar in an electric mixing bowl or food processor. Add the egg substitute and blend well.

4. Add the powdered milk mixture, sour cream, margarine, and flour, mixing until the batter is smooth and well-combined. Stir in the lemon juice and vanilla by hand.

5. Remove the springform pan from the freezer. Pour the batter into the pan and smooth with a rubber spatula.

6. Place the pan on the center rack of the oven and bake until the cheesecake sets and is lightly brown. If the cake begins to brown too quickly, cover the top loosely with aluminum foil. The cheesecake is done when the center of the cake is firm to the touch.

7. Remove the cake from the oven and place on a wire rack until completely cool (about 2 hours). Once cool, refrigerate for at least 2 hours. When chilled, the cheesecake will come out of the pan easily.

8. Before removing the pan, loosen the cake from the sides with a knife or metal spatula.

9. Cut into wedges and serve.

Basic Tofu Cheesecake

INGREDIENT	FOR 6-INCH CAKE	FOR 9-INCH CAKE
Fat-free cream cheese, softened	2 8-ounce packages	4 8-ounce packages
Firm tofu, mashed	8 ounces	16 ounces
Sugar	¾ cup	1½ cups
Fat-free egg substitute	4 ounces	8 ounces
Nonfat powdered milk	¼ cup mixed with 2 tablespoons water	½ cup mixed with ¼ cup water
Fat-free sour cream	¼ cup	½ cup
Fat-free yogurt	¼ cup	½ cup
Fresh lemon juice	1 tablespoon	2 tablespoons
Vanilla extract	1 teaspoon	2 teaspoons
CRUST		
Graham Cracker (page 8)	single recipe	double recipe

Baking Time	45–60 minutes	1¼–1½ hours
Serves	8	16
Calories per serving	184 (15 from fat)	184 (15 from fat)
Fat per serving	1.75 grams	1.75 grams

Attractive because of its nutritional qualities, tofu is high in protein and calcium, and contains all eight essential amino acids. When preparing this cheesecake, use the freshest tofu available.

---

1. Preheat the oven to 350°F.

2. Gently pat the prepared crust mixture on the bottom and partially up the sides of a greased springform pan. Place in the freezer for 10 minutes.

3. Blend the cream cheese, tofu, and sugar in an electric mixing bowl or food processor. Add the egg substitute and blend well.

4. Add the powdered milk mixture, sour cream, and yogurt, mixing until the batter is smooth and well-combined. Stir in the lemon juice and vanilla by hand.

5. Remove the springform pan from the freezer. Pour the batter into the pan and smooth with a rubber spatula.

6. Place the pan on the center rack of the oven and bake until the cheesecake sets and is lightly brown. If the cake begins to brown too quickly, cover the top loosely with aluminum foil. The cheesecake is done when the center of the cake is firm to the touch.

7. Remove the cake from the oven and place on a wire rack until completely cool (about 2 hours). Once cool, refrigerate for at least 2 hours. When chilled, the cheesecake will come out of the pan easily.

8. Before removing the pan, loosen the cake from the sides with a knife or metal spatula.

9. Cut into wedges and serve.

Basic Fat-Free Ricotta Cheesecake

INGREDIENT	FOR 6-INCH CAKE	FOR 9-INCH CAKE
Fat-free ricotta cheese	16 ounces	32 ounces
Sugar	¾ cup	1½ cups
Fat-free egg substitute	8 ounces	16 ounces
Nonfat powdered milk	¼ cup mixed with 2 tablespoons water	½ cup mixed with ¼ cup water
Fat-free sour cream	½ cup	1 cup
Fat-free margarine, melted	¼ cup	½ cup
All-purpose flour	¼ cup	½ cup
Fresh lemon juice	1 tablespoon	2 tablespoons
Vanilla extract	1 teaspoon	2 teaspoons
CRUST		
Graham Cracker (page 8)	single recipe	double recipe

Baking Time	45–60 minutes	1¼–1½ hours
Serves	8	16
Calories per serving	209	209
Fat per serving	0 gram	0 gram

Here's a variation of traditional Italian-style cheesecake, which uses ricotta cheese. Because of the texture of the ricotta, I find a food processor works best to blend the filling ingredients.

1. Preheat the oven to 350°F.

2. Gently pat the prepared crust mixture on the bottom and partially up the sides of a greased springform pan. Place in the freezer for 10 minutes.

3. Blend the ricotta cheese and sugar in a food processor. Add the egg substitute and blend well.

4. Add the powdered milk mixture, sour cream, margarine, and flour, mixing until the batter is smooth and well-combined. Stir in the lemon juice and vanilla by hand.

5. Remove the springform pan from the freezer. Pour the batter into the pan and smooth with a rubber spatula.

6. Place the pan on the center rack of the oven and bake until the cheesecake sets and is lightly brown. If the cake begins to brown too quickly, cover the top loosely with aluminum foil. The cheesecake is done when the center of the cake is firm to the touch.

7. Remove the cake from the oven and place on a wire rack until completely cool (about 2 hours). Once cool, refrigerate for at least 2 hours. When chilled, the cheesecake will come out of the pan easily.

8. Before removing the pan, loosen the cake from the sides with a knife or metal spatula.

9. Cut into wedges and serve.

Basic Lactose-Free Cheesecake

INGREDIENT	FOR 6-INCH CAKE	FOR 9-INCH CAKE
Firm tofu, mashed	1 cup	2 cups
Tahini*	½ cup	1 cup
Chick peas, mashed	½ cup	1 cup
Sugar	¾ cup	1½ cups
Soy milk	1 cup	2 cups
Fat-free margarine, melted	¼ cup	½ cup
All-purpose flour	¼ cup	½ cup
Fresh lemon juice	1 teaspoon	2 teaspoons
Vanilla extract	1 teaspoon	2 teaspoons
CRUST		
Graham Cracker (page 8)	single recipe	double recipe

* Tahini (puréed sesame seeds) is available in most supermarkets.

Baking Time	45–60 minutes	1¼–1½ hours
Serves	8	16
Calories per serving	233 (45 from fat)	233 (45 from fat)
Fat per serving	5 grams	5 grams

Even if you are lactose intolerant, you can still enjoy the rich creamy goodness of cheesecake. I have found that a food processor works best to blend the filling ingredients for this recipe.

---

1. Preheat the oven to 350°F.

2. Gently pat the prepared crust mixture on the bottom and partially up the sides of a greased springform pan. Place in the freezer for 10 minutes.

3. Blend the tofu, tahini, chick peas, and sugar in a food processor.

4. Add the soy milk, margarine, and flour, mixing until the batter is smooth and well-combined. Stir in the lemon juice and vanilla by hand.

5. Remove the springform pan from the freezer. Pour the batter into the pan, and smooth with a rubber spatula.

6. Place the pan on the center rack of the oven and bake until the cheesecake sets and is lightly brown. If the cake begins to brown too quickly, cover the top loosely with aluminum foil. The cheesecake is done when the center of the cake is firm to the touch.

7. Remove the cake from the oven and place on a wire rack until completely cool (about 2 hours). Once cool, refrigerate for at least 2 hours. When chilled, the cheesecake will come out of the pan easily.

8. Loosen the cheesecake from the sides of the pan with a knife or metal spatula before removing it.

9. Cut into wedges and serve.

Making Chocolate-Dipped Cheesecake Wedges

Freezing a wedge of your favorite cheesecake, then dipping it in chocolate can raise any cheesecake flavor to new taste-tempting heights. The following instructions are for a 6-inch cake. Double the chocolate for a 9-inch cake.

1. Freeze your favorite cheesecake. Using a sharp knife, cut the cake into wedges and refreeze another ten minutes.

2. Melt 8 to 10 ounces of good-quality chocolate in a double boiler, stirring until it is completely melted and smooth.

3. Using a metal slotted spoon, dip each frozen cheesecake slice in chocolate, turning to coat evenly. Let the excess chocolate drain through the spoon.

4. Place the dipped slices on a wax paper-lined cookie sheet and place in the refrigerator for at least one hour to set the chocolate.

4.

Light and Fruity Cheesecakes

L emons, cherries, and strawberries are just a few of the fruits found in this chapter's delightful cheese-cake creations. In addition to basic fruit-flavored varieties, you can choose from such unique selections as Honey Tangerine (page 64), Papaya Passion (page 72), and Raspberry Royale (page 60). If you like the taste of pineapple and rum, be sure to try the tropical Piña Colada Cheesecake (page 52) complete with a coconut-flavored crust. All are perfect to serve as cool summer treats or as finales to warm winter meals.

Luscious Lemon Cheesecake

INGREDIENT	FOR 6-INCH CAKE	FOR 9-INCH CAKE
Fat-free cream cheese, softened	3 8-ounce packages	6 8-ounce packages
Sugar	¾ cup	1½ cups
Fat-free egg substitute	4 ounces	8 ounces
Nonfat powdered milk	¼ cup mixed with 2 tablespoons water	½ cup mixed with ¼ cup water
Fat-free sour cream	¼ cup	½ cup
Fat-free margarine, melted	¼ cup	½ cup
All-purpose flour	¼ cup	½ cup
Fresh lemon juice	⅓ cup	⅔ cup
Grated lemon zest	2 teaspoons	4 teaspoons
Pure lemon extract	1 teaspoon	2 teaspoons
CRUST		
Lemony Graham Cracker (page 14)	single recipe	double recipe
GARNISH		
Low-fat whipped topping	1 cup	2 cups
Grated lemon zest	1 tablespoon	2 tablespoons

Baking Time	45–60 minutes	1¼–1½ hours
Serves	8	16
Calories per serving	223 (9 from fat)	223 (9 from fat)
Fat per serving	1 gram	1 gram

Light and cool, this lemony cheesecake adds just the right touch to a special brunch or a light supper.

---

1. Preheat the oven to 350°F.

2. Gently pat the prepared crust mixture on the bottom and partially up the sides of a greased springform pan. Place in the freezer for 10 minutes.

3. Blend the cream cheese and sugar in an electric mixing bowl or food processor. Add the egg substitute and blend well.

4. Add the powdered milk mixture, sour cream, margarine, and flour, mixing until the batter is smooth and well-combined. Stir in the lemon juice, zest, and extract by hand.

5. Remove the springform pan from the freezer. Pour the batter into the pan and smooth with a rubber spatula.

6. Place the pan on the center rack of the oven and bake until the cheesecake sets and is lightly brown. If the cake begins to brown too quickly, cover the top loosely with aluminum foil. The cheesecake is done when the center of the cake is firm to the touch.

7. Remove the cake from the oven and place on a wire rack until completely cool (about 2 hours). Once cool, refrigerate the cake for at least 2 hours. When chilled, the cheesecake will come out of the pan easily.

8. Before removing the pan, loosen the cake from the sides with a knife or metal spatula.

9. Spoon the topping into a pastry bag and pipe it along the top edge of the cake. Sprinkle with lemon zest.

10. Cut into wedges and serve.

Tangy Lime Cheesecake

INGREDIENT	FOR 6-INCH CAKE	FOR 9-INCH CAKE
Fat-free cream cheese, softened	3 8-ounce packages	6 8-ounce packages
Sugar	¾ cup	1½ cups
Fat-free egg substitute	4 ounces	8 ounces
Nonfat powdered milk	¼ cup mixed with 2 tablespoons water	½ cup mixed with ¼ cup water
Fat-free sour cream	¼ cup	½ cup
Fat-free margarine, melted	¼ cup	½ cup
All-purpose flour	¼ cup	½ cup
Fresh lime juice	⅓ cup	⅔ cup
Grated lime zest	2 teaspoons	4 teaspoons
Pure lime extract	1 teaspoon	2 teaspoons

CRUST

Zesty Lime Graham Cracker (page 16)	single recipe	double recipe

GARNISH

Low-fat whipped topping	1 cup	2 cups
Lime zest	1 tablespoon	2 tablespoons

Baking Time	45–60 minutes	1¼–1½ hours
Serves	8	16
Calories per serving	223 (9 from fat)	223 (9 from fat)
Fat per serving	1 gram	1 gram

For added color, fold a drop or two of green food coloring into the batter.

---

1. Preheat the oven to 350°F.

2. Gently pat the prepared crust mixture on the bottom and partially up the sides of a greased springform pan. Place in the freezer for 10 minutes.

3. Blend the cream cheese and sugar in an electric mixing bowl or food processor. Add the egg substitute and blend well.

4. Add the powdered milk mixture, sour cream, margarine, and flour, mixing until the batter is smooth and well-combined. Stir in the lime juice, zest, and extract by hand.

5. Remove the springform pan from the freezer. Pour the batter into the pan and smooth with a rubber spatula.

6. Place the pan on the center rack of the oven and bake until the cheesecake sets and is lightly brown. If the cake begins to brown too quickly, cover the top loosely with aluminum foil. The cheesecake is done when the center of the cake is firm to the touch.

7. Remove the cake from the oven and place on a wire rack until completely cool (about 2 hours). Once cool, refrigerate the cake for at least 2 hours. When chilled, the cheesecake will come out of the pan easily.

8. Before removing the pan, loosen the cake from the sides with a knife or metal spatula.

9. Spoon the topping into a pastry bag and pipe it decoratively on the cake. Sprinkle with lime zest.

10. Cut into wedges and serve.

Piña Colada Cheesecake

INGREDIENT	FOR 6-INCH CAKE	FOR 9-INCH CAKE
Fat-free cream cheese, softened	3 8-ounce packages	6 8-ounce packages
Sugar	¾ cup	1½ cups
Fat-free egg substitute	4 ounces	8 ounces
Nonfat powdered milk	¼ cup mixed with 2 tablespoons water	½ cup mixed with ¼ cup water
Fat-free sour cream	¼ cup	½ cup
Fat-free margarine, melted	¼ cup	½ cup
All-purpose flour	¼ cup	½ cup
Coconut extract	1 teaspoon	2 teaspoons
Rum extract	1 teaspoon	2 teaspoons
Crushed pineapple, drained	1 cup	2 cups

CRUST

Coconut Graham Cracker (page 20)	single recipe	double recipe

GARNISH

Low-fat whipped topping	1 cup	2 cups
Pineapple rings, halved	4	8
Flaked coconut	1 teaspoon	2 teaspoons

Baking Time	45–60 minutes	1 ¼–1½ hours
Serves	8	16
Calories per serving	216 (9 from fat)	216 (9 from fat)
Fat per serving	1 gram	1 gram

The flavors found in a classic piña colada—pineapple, coconut, and rum—make a truly wonderful cheesecake.

---

1. Preheat the oven to 350°F.

2. Gently pat the prepared crust mixture on the bottom and partially up the sides of a greased springform pan. Place in the freezer for 10 minutes.

3. Blend the cream cheese and sugar in an electric mixing bowl or food processor. Add the egg substitute and blend well.

4. Add the powdered milk mixture, sour cream, margarine, and flour, mixing until the batter is smooth and well-combined. Stir in the coconut and rum extracts by hand. Fold in the crushed pineapple.

5. Remove the springform pan from the freezer. Pour the batter into the pan and smooth with a rubber spatula.

6. Place the pan on the center rack of the oven and bake until the cheesecake sets and is lightly brown. If the cake begins to brown too quickly, cover the top loosely with aluminum foil. The cheesecake is done when the center of the cake is firm to the touch.

7. Remove the cake from the oven and place on a wire rack until completely cool (about 2 hours). Once cool, refrigerate the cake for at least 2 hours. When chilled, the cheesecake will come out of the pan easily.

8. Before removing the pan, loosen the cake from the sides with a knife or metal spatula.

9. Arrange the pineapple halves decoratively on top of the cheesecake. Spoon the whipped topping into a pastry bag and pipe it between the pineapple. Sprinkle with coconut.

10. Cut into wedges and serve.

Classic Cherry Cheesecake

INGREDIENT	FOR 6-INCH CAKE	FOR 9-INCH CAKE
Fat-free cream cheese, softened	2 8-ounce packages	4 8-ounce packages
Firm tofu, mashed	8 ounces	16 ounces
Sugar	¾ cup	1½ cups
Fat-free egg substitute	4 ounces	8 ounces
Nonfat powdered milk	¼ cup mixed with 2 tablespoons water	½ cup mixed with ¼ cup water
Fat-free sour cream	¼ cup	½ cup
Fat-free yogurt	¼ cup	½ cup
Cherry juice	¼ cup	½ cup
Cherry extract	1 teaspoon	2 teaspoons
Vanilla extract	1 teaspoon	2 teaspoons
Dark sweet cherries, halved	1 cup	2 cups

CRUST

Chewy Oat (page 22)	single recipe	double recipe

GARNISH

Low-fat whipped topping	1 cup	2 cups
Dark sweet cherries	8	16

Baking Time	45–60 minutes	1¼–1½ hours
Serves	8	16
Calories per serving	240 (25 from fat)	240 (25 from fat)
Fat per serving	2.75 grams	2.75 grams

Cherry is one of my husband's favorite flavors, so I created this cheesecake just for him. Be sure to try it with any of the basic cheesecake recipes found in Chapter 3.

---

1. Preheat the oven to 350°F.

2. Gently pat the prepared crust mixture on the bottom and partially up the sides of a greased springform pan. Place in the freezer for 10 minutes.

3. Blend the cream cheese, tofu, and sugar in an electric mixer or food processor. Add the egg substitute and blend well.

4. Add the powdered milk mixture, sour cream, yogurt, and cherry juice, mixing until the batter is smooth and well-combined. Stir in the cherry and vanilla extracts by hand. Gently fold in the cherries.

5. Remove the springform pan from the freezer. Pour the batter into the pan and smooth with a rubber spatula.

6. Place the pan on the center rack of the oven and bake until the cheesecake sets and is lightly brown. If the cake begins to brown too quickly, cover the top loosely with aluminum foil. The cheesecake is done when the center of the cake is firm to the touch.

7. Remove the cake from the oven and place on a wire rack until completely cool (about 2 hours). Once cool, refrigerate the cake for at least 2 hours. When chilled, the cheesecake will come out of the pan easily.

8. Before removing the pan, loosen the cake from the sides with a knife or metal spatula.

9. Spoon the whipped topping into a pastry bag and pipe rosettes along the edge of the cheesecake. Place a cherry on top of each rosette.

10. Cut into wedges and serve.

Simply Strawberry Cheesecake

INGREDIENT	FOR 6-INCH CAKE	FOR 9-INCH CAKE
Fat-free cream cheese, softened	2 8-ounce packages	4 8-ounce packages
Firm tofu, mashed	8 ounces	16 ounces
Sugar	¾ cup	1½ cups
Fat-free egg substitute	4 ounces	8 ounces
Nonfat powdered milk	¼ cup mixed with 2 tablespoons water	½ cup mixed with ¼ cup water
Fat-free sour cream	¼ cup	½ cup
Fat-free yogurt	¼ cup	½ cup
Vanilla extract	1 teaspoon	2 teaspoons
Sliced strawberries, fresh or frozen*	½ cup	1 cup
CRUST		
Graham Cracker (page 8)	single recipe	double recipe
GARNISH		
Low-fat whipped topping	1 cup	2 cups
Sliced fresh strawberries	8	16

* Be sure to thaw and drain if using frozen variety.

Baking Time	45–60 minutes	1¼–1½ hours
Serves	8	16
Calories per serving	230 (25 from fat)	230 (25 from fat)
Fat per serving	2.75 grams	2.75 grams

Sweet strawberries have a starring role in this great-tasting cheesecake.

---

1. Preheat the oven to 350°F.

2. Gently pat the prepared crust mixture on the bottom and partially up the sides of a greased springform pan. Place in the freezer for 10 minutes.

3. Blend the cream cheese, tofu, and sugar in an electric mixer or food processor. Add the egg substitute and blend well.

4. Add the powdered milk mixture, sour cream, and yogurt, mixing until the batter is smooth and well-combined. Stir in the vanilla by hand. Gently fold in the strawberries.

5. Remove the springform pan from the freezer. Pour the batter into the pan and smooth with a rubber spatula.

6. Place the pan on the center rack of the oven and bake until the cheesecake sets and is lightly brown. If the cake begins to brown too quickly, cover the top loosely with aluminum foil. The cheesecake is done when the center of the cake is firm to the touch.

7. Remove the cake from the oven and place on a wire rack until completely cool (about 2 hours). Once cool, refrigerate the cake for at least 2 hours. When chilled, the cheesecake will come out of the pan easily.

8. Before removing the pan, loosen the cake from the sides with a knife or metal spatula.

9. Spoon the whipped topping into a pastry bag and pipe rosettes along the edge of the cheesecake. Place a strawberry slice on top of each rosette. Arrange the remaining strawberry slices in a fan shape in the middle of the cheesecake.

10. Cut into wedges and serve.

Basic Blackberry Cheesecake

INGREDIENT	FOR 6-INCH CAKE	FOR 9-INCH CAKE
Fat-free cream cheese, softened	2 8-ounce packages	4 8-ounce packages
Firm tofu, mashed	8 ounces	16 ounces
Sugar	¾ cup	1½ cups
Fat-free egg substitute	4 ounces	8 ounces
Nonfat powdered milk	¼ cup mixed with 2 tablespoons water	½ cup mixed with ¼ cup water
Fat-free sour cream	¼ cup	½ cup
Fat-free yogurt	¼ cup	½ cup
Vanilla extract	1 teaspoon	2 teaspoons
Puréed blackberries, fresh or frozen*	½ cup	1 cup

CRUST

Graham Cracker (page 8)	single recipe	double recipe

GARNISH

Low-fat whipped topping	1 cup	2 cups
Fresh blackberries	8	16

* Be sure to thaw and drain if using frozen variety.

Baking Time	45–60 minutes	1¼–1½ hours
Serves	8	16
Calories per serving	230 (25 from fat)	230 (25 from fat)
Fat per serving	2.75 grams	2.75 grams

Whether you use fresh or frozen blackberries, this cheesecake is sensational.

1. Preheat the oven to 350°F.

2. Gently pat the prepared crust mixture on the bottom and partially up the sides of a greased springform pan. Place in the freezer for 10 minutes.

3. Blend the cream cheese, tofu, and sugar in an electric mixer or food processor. Add the egg substitute and blend well.

4. Add the powdered milk mixture, sour cream, and yogurt, mixing until the batter is smooth and well-combined. Stir in the vanilla by hand. Gently fold in the blackberries.

5. Remove the springform pan from the freezer. Pour the batter into the pan and smooth with a rubber spatula.

6. Place the pan on the center rack of the oven and bake until the cheesecake sets and is lightly brown. If the cake begins to brown too quickly, cover the top loosely with aluminum foil. The cheesecake is done when the center of the cake is firm to the touch.

7. Remove the cake from the oven and place on a wire rack until completely cool (about 2 hours). Once cool, refrigerate the cake for at least 2 hours. When chilled, the cheesecake will come out of the pan easily.

8. Before removing the pan, loosen the cake from the sides with a knife or metal spatula.

9. Spoon the whipped topping into a pastry bag and pipe rosettes along the edge of the cheesecake. Place a blackberry on top of each rosette.

10. Cut into wedges and serve.

Raspberry Royale Cheesecake

INGREDIENT	FOR 6-INCH CAKE	FOR 9-INCH CAKE
Fat-free cream cheese, softened	2 8-ounce packages	4 8-ounce packages
Firm tofu, mashed	8 ounces	16 ounces
Sugar	¾ cup	1½ cups
Fat-free egg substitute	4 ounces	8 ounces
Nonfat powdered milk	¼ cup mixed with 2 tablespoons water	½ cup mixed with ¼ cup water
Fat-free sour cream	¼ cup	½ cup
Fat-free yogurt	¼ cup	½ cup
Vanilla extract	1 teaspoon	2 teaspoons
Puréed raspberries, fresh or frozen*	½ cup	1 cup

CRUST

Graham Cracker (page 8)	single recipe	double recipe

GARNISH

Low-fat whipped topping	1 cup	2 cups
Fresh raspberries	8	16

* Be sure to thaw and drain if using frozen variety.

Baking Time	45–60 minutes	1¼–1½ hours
Serves	8	16
Calories per serving	230 (25 from fat)	230 (25 from fat)
Fat per serving	2.75 grams	2.75 grams

This simple, elegant cheesecake is fit for royalty.

---

1. Preheat the oven to 350°F.

2. Gently pat the prepared crust mixture on the bottom and partially up the sides of a greased springform pan. Place in the freezer for 10 minutes.

3. Blend the cream cheese, tofu, and sugar in an electric mixer or food processor. Add the egg substitute and blend well.

4. Add the powdered milk mixture, sour cream, and yogurt, mixing until the batter is smooth and well-combined. Stir in the vanilla by hand. Gently fold in the raspberries.

5. Remove the springform pan from the freezer. Pour the batter into the pan and smooth with a rubber spatula.

6. Place the pan on the center rack of the oven and bake until the cheesecake sets and is lightly brown. If the cake begins to brown too quickly, cover the top loosely with aluminum foil. The cheesecake is done when the center of the cake is firm to the touch.

7. Remove the cake from the oven and place on a wire rack until completely cool (about 2 hours). Once cool, refrigerate the cake for at least 2 hours. When chilled, the cheesecake will come out of the pan easily.

8. Before removing the pan, loosen the cake from the sides with a knife or metal spatula.

9. Spoon the whipped topping into a pastry bag and pipe rosettes along the edge of the cheesecake. Place a raspberry on top of each rosette.

10. Cut into wedges and serve.

Blueberry Deluxe Cheesecake

INGREDIENT	FOR 6-INCH CAKE	FOR 9-INCH CAKE
Fat-free cream cheese, softened	3 8-ounce packages	6 8-ounce packages
Sugar	¾ cup	1½ cups
Fat-free egg substitute	4 ounces	8 ounces
Nonfat powdered milk	¼ cup mixed with 2 tablespoons water	½ cup mixed with ¼ cup water
Fat-free sour cream	¼ cup	½ cup
Fat-free margarine, melted	¼ cup	½ cup
All-purpose flour	¼ cup	½ cup
Fresh lemon juice	1 tablespoon	2 tablespoons
Vanilla extract	1 teaspoon	2 teaspoons
Fresh blueberries	½ cup	1 cup

CRUST

Graham Cracker (page 8)	single recipe	double recipe

GARNISH

Low-fat whipped topping	1 cup	2 cups
Fresh blueberries	½ cup	1 cup

Baking Time	45–60 minutes	1¼ –1½ hours
Serves	8	16
Calories per serving	185 (9 from fat)	185 (9 from fat)
Fat per serving	1 gram	1 gram

When blueberries are in season, be sure to make this fabulous cheesecake.

---

1. Preheat the oven to 350°F.

2. Gently pat the prepared crust mixture on the bottom and partially up the sides of a greased springform pan. Place in the freezer for 10 minutes.

3. Blend the cream cheese and sugar in an electric mixing bowl or food processor. Add the egg substitute and blend well.

4. Add the powdered milk mixture, sour cream, margarine, and flour, mixing until the batter is smooth and well-combined. Stir in the lemon juice and vanilla by hand. Gently fold in the blueberries.

5. Remove the springform pan from the freezer. Pour the batter into the pan and smooth with a rubber spatula.

6. Place the pan on the center rack of the oven and bake until the cheesecake sets and is lightly brown. If the cake begins to brown too quickly, cover the top loosely with aluminum foil. The cheesecake is done when the center of the cake is firm to the touch.

7. Remove the cake from the oven and place on a wire rack until completely cool (about 2 hours). Once cool, refrigerate the cake for at least 2 hours. When chilled, the cheesecake will come out of the pan easily.

8. Before removing the pan, loosen the cake from the sides with a knife or metal spatula.

9. Spoon the topping into a pastry bag and pipe it decoratively on top of the cake. Sprinkle with fresh blueberries.

10. Cut into wedges and serve.

Honey Tangerine Cheesecake

INGREDIENT	FOR 6-INCH CAKE	FOR 9-INCH CAKE
Fat-free cream cheese, softened	3 8-ounce packages	6 8-ounce packages
Honey	½ cup	1 cup
Fat-free egg substitute	4 ounces	8 ounces
Nonfat powdered milk	¼ cup mixed with 2 tablespoons water	½ cup mixed with ¼ cup water
Fat-free sour cream	¼ cup	½ cup
Fat-free margarine, melted	¼ cup	½ cup
All-purpose flour	¼ cup	½ cup
Fresh lemon juice	1 tablespoon	2 tablespoons
Vanilla extract	1 teaspoon	2 teaspoons
Puréed tangerines	½ cup	1 cup
Grated tangerine zest	1 teaspoon	2 teaspoons
CRUST		
Graham Cracker (page 8)	single recipe	double recipe
GARNISH		
Low-fat whipped topping	1 cup	2 cups
Grated tangerine zest	1 tablespoon	2 tablespoons

Baking Time	45–60 minutes	1¼–1½ hours
Serves	8	16
Calories per serving	240 (9 from fat)	240 (9 from fat)
Fat per serving	1 gram	1 gram

Top: Chocolate and Cream Cheesecake (page 158)

Center Left: Chocolate-dipped cheesecake wedge (page 46)

Center Right: Basic Fat-Free Cheesecake (page 38)

Bottom: Simply Strawberry Cheesecake (page 56)

Top Right and Bottom Left: Triple Treat Cheesecake (page 156)

Center Left: Honey Tangerine Cheesecake (page 64)

Center Right: Chocolate Chip Cheesecake (page 80)

The fruity flavor of fresh tangerines gives this cheesecake a decidedly different twist.

---

1. Preheat the oven to 350°F.

2. Gently pat the prepared crust mixture on the bottom and partially up the sides of a greased springform pan. Place in the freezer for 10 minutes.

3. Blend the cream cheese and honey in an electric mixing bowl or food processor. Add the egg substitute and blend well.

4. Add the powdered milk mixture, sour cream, margarine, and flour, mixing until the batter is smooth and well-combined. Stir in the lemon juice and vanilla by hand. Gently fold in the tangerines and zest.

5. Remove the springform pan from the freezer. Pour the batter into the pan and smooth with a rubber spatula.

6. Place the pan on the center rack of the oven and bake until the cheesecake sets and is lightly brown. If the cake begins to brown too quickly, cover the top loosely with aluminum foil. The cheesecake is done when the center of the cake is firm to the touch.

7. Remove the cake from the oven and place on a wire rack until completely cool (about 2 hours). Once cool, refrigerate the cake for at least 2 hours. When chilled, the cheesecake will come out of the pan easily.

8. Before removing the pan, loosen the cake from the sides with a knife or metal spatula.

9. Spoon the topping into a pastry bag and pipe it decoratively on top of the cake. Sprinkle with tangerine zest.

10. Cut into wedges and serve.

Heavenly Apricot Cheesecake

INGREDIENT	FOR 6-INCH CAKE	FOR 9-INCH CAKE
Fat-free cream cheese, softened	3 8-ounce packages	6 8-ounce packages
Honey	½ cup	1 cup
Fat-free egg substitute	4 ounces	8 ounces
Nonfat powdered milk	¼ cup mixed with 2 tablespoons water	½ cup mixed with ¼ cup water
Fat-free sour cream	¼ cup	½ cup
Fat-free margarine, melted	¼ cup	½ cup
All-purpose flour	¼ cup	½ cup
Fresh lemon juice	1 tablespoon	2 tablespoons
Vanilla extract	1 teaspoon	2 teaspoons
Puréed apricots	½ cup	1 cup
CRUST		
Graham Cracker (page 8)	single recipe	double recipe
GARNISH		
Low-fat whipped topping	1 cup	2 cups
Apricot slices	8	16

Baking Time	45–60 minutes	1¼–1½ hours
Serves	8	16
Calories per serving	240 (9 from fat)	240 (9 from fat)
Fat per serving	1 gram	1 gram

Fresh, sweet apricots are spotlighted in this luscious cheesecake.

---

1. Preheat the oven to 350°F.

2. Gently pat the prepared crust mixture on the bottom and partially up the sides of a greased springform pan. Place in the freezer for 10 minutes.

3. Blend the cream cheese and honey in an electric mixing bowl or food processor. Add the egg substitute and blend well.

4. Add the powdered milk mixture, sour cream, margarine, and flour, mixing until the batter is smooth and well-combined. Stir in the lemon juice and vanilla by hand. Gently fold in the apricots.

5. Remove the springform pan from the freezer. Pour the batter into the pan and smooth with a rubber spatula.

6. Place the pan on the center rack of the oven and bake until the cheesecake sets and is lightly brown. If the cake begins to brown too quickly, cover the top loosely with aluminum foil. The cheesecake is done when the center of the cake is firm to the touch.

7. Remove the cake from the oven and place on a wire rack until completely cool (about 2 hours). Once cool, refrigerate the cake for at least 2 hours. When chilled, the cheesecake will come out of the pan easily.

8. Before removing the pan, loosen the cake from the sides with a knife or metal spatula.

9. Spoon the topping into a pastry bag and pipe it decoratively on top of the cake. Arrange the apricot slices on top.

10. Cut into wedges and serve.

Incredible Grape Cheesecake

INGREDIENT	FOR 6-INCH CAKE	FOR 9-INCH CAKE
Fat-free cream cheese, softened	3 8-ounce packages	6 8-ounce packages
Sugar	¾ cup	1½ cups
Fat-free egg substitute	4 ounces	8 ounces
Nonfat powdered milk	¼ cup mixed with 2 tablespoons water	½ cup mixed with ¼ cup water
Fat-free sour cream	¼ cup	½ cup
Fat-free margarine, melted	¼ cup	½ cup
White or purple grape juice concentrate*	6 ounces	12 ounces
All-prupose flour	¼ cup	½ cup
Fresh lemon juice	1 tablespoon	2 tablespoons
Vanilla extract	1 teaspoon	2 teaspoons
CRUST		
Graham Cracker (page 8)	single recipe	double recipe
GARNISH		
Low-fat topping	1 cup	2 cups
Green or purple grapes	8	16

* Be sure to thaw if using frozen variety.

Baking Time	45–60 minutes	1¼–1½ hours
Serves	8	16
Calories per serving	244 (9 from fat)	244 (9 from fat)
Fat per serving	1 gram	1 gram

Here is a cheesecake flavor for the adventurous spirit. Different, yes; but amazingly good.

---

1. Preheat the oven to 350°F.

2. Gently pat the prepared crust mixture on the bottom and partially up the sides of a greased springform pan. Place in the freezer for 10 minutes.

3. Blend the cream cheese and sugar in an electric mixing bowl or food processor. Add the egg substitute and blend well.

4. Add the powdered milk mixture, sour cream, margarine, grape juice, and flour, mixing until the batter is smooth and well-combined. Stir in the lemon juice and vanilla by hand.

5. Remove the springform pan from the freezer. Pour the batter into the pan and smooth with a rubber spatula.

6. Place the pan on the center rack of the oven and bake until the cheesecake sets and is lightly brown. If the cake begins to brown too quickly, cover the top loosely with aluminum foil. The cheesecake is done when the center of the cake is firm to the touch.

7. Remove the cake from the oven and place on a wire rack until completely cool (about 2 hours). Once cool, refrigerate the cake for at least 2 hours. When chilled, the cheesecake will come out of the pan easily.

8. Before removing the pan, loosen the cake from the sides with a knife or metal spatula.

9. Spoon the whipped topping into a pastry bag and pipe rosettes along the edge of the cheesecake. Place a grape on top of each rosette.

10. Cut into wedges and serve.

Mango Supreme Cheesecake

INGREDIENT	FOR 6-INCH CAKE	FOR 9-INCH CAKE
Fat-free ricotta cheese	16 ounces	32 ounces
Sugar	¾ cup	1½ cups
Fat-free egg substitute	8 ounces	16 ounces
Nonfat powdered milk	¼ cup mixed with 2 tablespoons water	½ cup mixed with ¼ cup water
Fat-free sour cream	½ cup	1 cup
Fat-free margarine, melted	¼ cup	½ cup
All-purpose flour	¼ cup	½ cup
Fresh lemon juice	1 tablespoon	2 tablespoons
Vanilla extract	1 teaspoon	2 teaspoons
Puréed mango	1 cup	2 cups

CRUST

Coconut Graham Cracker (page 20)	single recipe	double recipe

GARNISH

Low-fat whipped topping	1 cup	2 cups
Ripe mango, peeled and sliced	1 small	2 small

Baking Time	45–60 minutes	1¼–1½ hours
Serves	8	16
Calories per serving	243 (9 from fat)	243 (9 from fat)
Fat per serving	1 gram	1 gram

If you like tropical fruits, this mango-flavored cheesecake will drive you wild!

---

1. Preheat the oven to 350°F.

2. Gently pat the prepared crust mixture on the bottom and partially up the sides of a greased springform pan. Place in the freezer for 10 minutes.

3. Blend the ricotta cheese and sugar in a food processor. Add the egg substitute and blend well.

4. Add the powdered milk mixture, sour cream, margarine, and flour, mixing until the batter is smooth and well-combined. Stir in the lemon juice and vanilla by hand. Gently fold in the mango.

5. Remove the springform pan from the freezer. Pour the batter into the pan and smooth with a rubber spatula.

6. Place the pan on the center rack of the oven and bake until the cheesecake sets and is lightly brown. If the cake begins to brown too quickly, cover the top loosely with aluminum foil. The cheesecake is done when the center of the cake is firm to the touch.

7. Remove the cake from the oven and place on a wire rack until completely cool (about 2 hours). Once cool, refrigerate the cake for at least 2 hours. When chilled, the cheesecake will come out of the pan easily.

8. Before removing the pan, loosen the cake from the sides with a knife or metal spatula.

9. Spoon the topping into a pastry bag and pipe it along the top edge of the cake. Arrange a circle of mango slices in the center.

10. Cut into wedges and serve.

Papaya Passion Cheesecake

INGREDIENT	FOR 6-INCH CAKE	FOR 9-INCH CAKE
Mashed firm tofu	1 cup	2 cups
Tahini*	½ cup	1 cup
Chick peas, mashed	½ cup	1 cup
Sugar	¾ cup	1½ cups
Soy milk	½ cup	1 cup
Fat-free margarine, melted	¼ cup	½ cup
All-purpose flour	¼ cup	½ cup
Fresh lemon juice	1 tablespoon	2 tablespoons
Vanilla extract	1 teaspoon	2 teaspoons
Puréed papaya	1 cup	2 cups
Chopped dried papaya	⅓ cup	⅔ cup
CRUST		
Coconut Graham Cracker (page 20)	single recipe	double recipe
GARNISH		
Low-fat whipped topping	1 cup	2 cups
Fresh papaya, peeled, seeded, and sliced	1 small	2 small

* Tahini (puréed sesame seeds) is available in most supermarkets.

Baking Time	45–60 minutes	1¼–1½ hours
Serves	8	16
Calories per serving	288 (57 from fat)	288 (57 from fat)
Fat per serving	6.4 grams	6.4 grams

There is simply no substitute for the tangy flavor of papaya. Fresh and dried papaya make this lactose-free cheesecake truly special.

---

1. Preheat the oven to 350°F.

2. Gently pat the prepared crust mixture on the bottom and partially up the sides of a greased springform pan. Place in the freezer for 10 minutes.

3. Blend the tofu, tahini, chick peas, and sugar in a food processor.

4. Add the soy milk, margarine, and flour, mixing until the batter is smooth and well-combined. Stir in the lemon juice and vanilla by hand. Gently fold in the puréed and dried papaya.

5. Remove the springform pan from the freezer. Pour the batter into the pan and smooth with a rubber spatula.

6. Place the pan on the center rack of the oven and bake until the cheesecake sets and is lightly brown. If the cake begins to brown too quickly, cover the top loosely with aluminum foil. The cheesecake is done when the center of the cake is firm to the touch.

7. Remove the cake from the oven and place on a wire rack until completely cool (about 2 hours). Once cool, refrigerate the cake for at least 2 hours. When chilled, the cheesecake will come out of the pan easily.

8. Before removing the pan, loosen the cake from the sides with a knife or metal spatula.

9. Spoon the topping into a pastry bag and pipe it decoratively on the cake. Arrange a circle of papaya slices in the center.

10. Cut into wedges and serve.

Flavorful Zest

The coarse outer layer of skin on a citrus fruit—the zest—is where its most flavorful oils are located. (This includes only the outermost colored part of the skin, not the inner white portion, which is bitter.) In addition to being called zest, it is also referred to as skin, peel, or rind. Zest adds distinctive flavor to foods, and, in this book, is generally used as a flavorful and decorative garnish.

You can remove the zest from a lemon, orange, lime, or other citrus fruit in a number of ways. One popular method is to use a hand grater. Gently grate the zest directly from the fruit. You can also remove the zest with a hand peeler, which will take off the zest in larger pieces. The pieces may have to be chopped up before they are used. Finally, you can use a zester. Similar to a hand peeler, a zester is smaller and designed specifically to remove zest. It really doesn't matter which method you use, just be careful not to include any of the skin's bitter white portion.

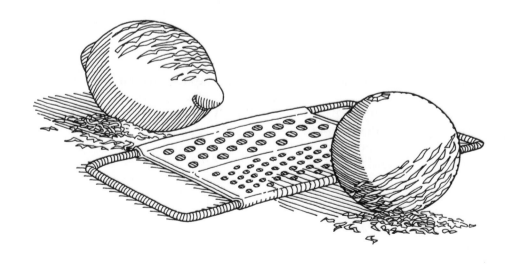

5.

Luscious Chocolate Creations

I have always been a chocolate lover. It is this passion that inspired me to create the irresistibly rich, chocolaty cheesecakes found in this chapter. They are among my favorites.

To make your chocolate cheesecakes both delicious and healthful, always use the best quality chocolate you can find. Choose varieties that have at least 25 percent cocoa solids (very good chocolate has up to 60 percent) and cocoa butter (not hydrogenated fat) on their list of ingredients. For low-fat chocolate recipes, use European-style cocoa instead of chocolate. It is richer than regular cocoa and lower in fat. Hershey's makes an excellent European-style cocoa that is readily available in most grocery stores. Carob —a lower-fat chocolate alternative—can be substituted for the cocoa in any recipe.

Have fun making and enjoying these chocolate delights. I hope you find them as delectable as I do.

Double Chocolate Cheesecake

INGREDIENT	FOR 6-INCH CAKE	FOR 9-INCH CAKE
Fat-free cream cheese, softened	3 8-ounce packages	6 8-ounce packages
Sugar	¾ cup	1½ cups
Fat-free egg substitute	4 ounces	8 ounces
Nonfat powdered milk	¼ cup mixed with 2 tablespoons water	½ cup mixed with ¼ cup water
Fat-free sour cream	¼ cup	½ cup
Fat-free margarine, melted	¼ cup	½ cup
European-style cocoa	½ cup	1 cup
All-purpose flour	¼ cup	½ cup
Fresh lemon juice	1 tablespoon	2 tablespoons
Vanilla extract	1 teaspoon	2 teaspoons
Mini chocolate chips	¼ cup	½ cup

CRUST

Chocolate Graham Cracker (page 10)	single recipe	double recipe

GARNISH

Low-fat whipped topping	1 cup	2 cups
European-style cocoa	1 teaspoon	2 teaspoons

Baking time	45–60 minutes	1¼–1½ hours
Serves	8	16
Calories per serving	251 (27 from fat)	251 (27 from fat)
Fat per serving	3 grams	3 grams

This luscious chocolaty cheesecake has lots of flavor but very little fat.

---

1. Preheat the oven to 350°F.

2. Gently pat the prepared crust mixture on the bottom and partially up the sides of a greased springform pan. Place in the freezer for 10 minutes.

3. Blend the cream cheese and sugar in an electric mixing bowl or food processor. Add the egg substitute and blend well.

4. Add the powdered milk mixture, sour cream, margarine, cocoa, and flour, mixing until the batter is smooth and well-combined. Stir in the lemon juice and vanilla by hand. Fold in the chocolate chips.

5. Remove the springform pan from the freezer. Pour the batter into the pan and smooth with a rubber spatula.

6. Place the pan on the center rack of the oven and bake until the cheesecake sets and is lightly brown. If the cake begins to brown too quickly, cover the top loosely with aluminum foil. The cheesecake is done when the center of the cake is firm to the touch.

7. Remove the cake from the oven and place on a wire rack until completely cool (about 2 hours). Once cool, refrigerate for at least 2 hours. When chilled, the cheesecake will come out of the pan easily.

8. Before removing the pan, loosen the cake from the sides with a knife or metal spatula.

9. Spoon the topping into a pastry bag and pipe it decoratively on top of the cake. Dust with cocoa.

10. Cut into wedges and serve.

Marble Swirl Cheesecake

INGREDIENT	FOR 6-INCH CAKE	FOR 9-INCH CAKE
Fat-free cream cheese, softened	3 8-ounce packages	6 8-ounce packages
Sugar	¾ cup	1½ cups
Fat-free egg substitute	4 ounces	8 ounces
Nonfat powdered milk	¼ cup mixed with 2 tablespoons water	½ cup mixed with ¼ cup water
Fat-free sour cream	¼ cup	½ cup
Fat-free margarine, melted	¼ cup	½ cup
All-purpose flour	¼ cup	½ cup
Fresh lemon juice	1 tablespoon	2 tablespoons
Vanilla extract	1 teaspoon	2 teaspoons
European-style cocoa	½ cup	1 cup
CRUST		
Chocolate Graham Cracker (page 10)	single recipe	double recipe
GARNISH		
Low-fat whipped topping	1 cup	2 cups
European-style cocoa	1 teaspoon	2 teaspoons

Baking time	45–60 minutes	1¼–1½ hours
Serves	8	16
Calories per serving	238 (20 from fat)	238 (20 from fat)
Fat per serving	2.2 grams	2.2 grams

Chocolate swirls in a sea of vanilla characterize this cheesecake classic.

---

1. Preheat the oven to 350°F.

2. Gently pat the prepared crust mixture on the bottom and partially up the sides of a greased springform pan. Place in the freezer for 10 minutes.

3. Blend the cream cheese and sugar in an electric mixing bowl or food processor. Add the egg substitute and blend well.

4. Add the powdered milk mixture, sour cream, margarine, and flour, mixing until the batter is smooth and well-combined. Stir in the lemon juice and vanilla by hand.

5. Remove the springform pan from the freezer. Pour two-thirds of the batter into the pan and smooth with a rubber spatula. Fold the cocoa into the remaining batter. Drop this chocolate batter onto the batter in the pan, and quickly run a spatula through it to form a marble pattern.

6. Place the pan on the center rack of the oven and bake until the cheesecake sets and is lightly brown. If the cake begins to brown too quickly, cover the top loosely with aluminum foil. The cheesecake is done when the center of the cake is firm to the touch.

7. Remove the cake from the oven and place on a wire rack until completely cool (about 2 hours). Once cool, refrigerate for at least 2 hours. When chilled, the cheesecake will come out of the pan easily.

8. Before removing the pan, loosen the cake from the sides with a knife or metal spatula.

9. Spoon the topping into a pastry bag and pipe it decoratively on top of the cake. Dust with cocoa.

10. Cut into wedges and serve.

Chocolate Chip Cheesecake

INGREDIENT	FOR 6-INCH CAKE	FOR 9-INCH CAKE
Fat-free cream cheese, softened	3 8-ounce packages	6 8-ounce packages
Sugar	¾ cup	1½ cups
Fat-free egg substitute	4 ounces	8 ounces
Nonfat powdered milk	¼ cup mixed with 2 tablespoons water	½ cup mixed with ¼ cup water
Fat-free sour cream	¼ cup	½ cup
Fat-free margarine, melted	¼ cup	½ cup
All-purpose flour	¼ cup	½ cup
Fresh lemon juice	1 tablespoon	2 tablespoons
Vanilla extract	1 teaspoon	2 teaspoons
Chocolate chips	¼ cup	½ cup

CRUST

Chocolate Graham Cracker (page 10)	single recipe	double recipe

GARNISH

Low-fat whipped topping	1 cup	2 cups
European-style cocoa	1 teaspoon	2 teaspoons

Baking time	45–60 minutes	1¼–1½ hours
Serves	8	16
Calories per serving	229 (14 from fat)	229 (14 from fat)
Fat per serving	1.5 grams	1.5 grams

For a black and white version of this cheesecake, use equal parts milk chocolate and white chocolate chips.

---

1. Preheat the oven to 350°F.

2. Gently pat the prepared crust mixture on the bottom and partially up the sides of a greased springform pan. Place in the freezer for 10 minutes.

3. Blend the cream cheese and sugar in an electric mixing bowl or food processor. Add the egg substitute and blend well.

4. Add the powdered milk mixture, sour cream, margarine, and flour, mixing until the batter is smooth and well-combined. Stir in the lemon juice and vanilla by hand. Fold in the chocolate chips.

5. Remove the springform pan from the freezer. Pour the batter into the pan and smooth with a rubber spatula.

6. Place the pan on the center rack of the oven and bake until the cheesecake sets and is lightly brown. If the cake begins to brown too quickly, cover the top loosely with aluminum foil. The cheesecake is done when the center of the cake is firm to the touch.

7. Remove the cake from the oven and place on a wire rack until completely cool (about 2 hours). Once cool, refrigerate for at least 2 hours. When chilled, the cheesecake will come out of the pan easily.

8. Before removing the pan, loosen the cake from the sides with a knife or metal spatula.

9. Spoon the topping into a pastry bag and pipe it decoratively on top of the cake. Dust with cocoa.

10. Cut into wedges and serve.

Classic Cocoa Cheesecake

INGREDIENT	FOR 6-INCH CAKE	FOR 9-INCH CAKE
Fat-free cream cheese, softened	3 8-ounce packages	6 8-ounce packages
Sugar	¾ cup	1½ cups
Fat-free egg substitute	4 ounces	8 ounces
Nonfat powdered milk	¼ cup mixed with 2 tablespoons water	½ cup mixed with ¼ cup water
Fat-free sour cream	¼ cup	½ cup
Fat-free margarine, melted	¼ cup	½ cup
European-style cocoa	½ cup	1 cup
All-purpose flour	¼ cup	½ cup
Fresh lemon juice	1 tablespoon	2 tablespoons
Vanilla extract	1 teaspoon	2 teaspoons

CRUST

Chocolate Graham Cracker (page 10)	single recipe	double recipe

GARNISH

Low-fat whipped topping	1 cup	2 cups
European-style cocoa	1 teaspoon	2 teaspoons

Baking time	45–60 minutes	1¼–1½ hours
Serves	8	16
Calories per serving	238 (20 from fat)	238 (20 from fat)
Fat per serving	2.2 grams	2.2 grams

Smooth, creamy, chocolaty cheesecake. What could be sweeter?

---

1. Preheat the oven to 350°F.

2. Gently pat the prepared crust mixture on the bottom and partially up the sides of a greased springform pan. Place in the freezer for 10 minutes.

3. Blend the cream cheese and sugar in an electric mixing bowl or food processor. Add the egg substitute and blend well.

4. Add the powdered milk mixture, sour cream, margarine, cocoa, and flour, mixing until the batter is smooth and well-combined. Stir in the lemon juice and vanilla by hand.

5. Remove the springform pan from the freezer. Pour the batter into the pan and smooth with a rubber spatula.

6. Place the pan on the center rack of the oven and bake until the cheesecake sets and is lightly brown. If the cake begins to brown too quickly, cover the top loosely with aluminum foil. The cheesecake is done when the center of the cake is firm to the touch.

7. Remove the cake from the oven and place on a wire rack until completely cool (about 2 hours). Once cool, refrigerate for at least 2 hours. When chilled, the cheesecake will come out of the pan easily.

8. Before removing the pan, loosen the cake from the sides with a knife or metal spatula.

9. Spoon the topping into a pastry bag and pipe it decoratively on top of the cake. Dust with cocoa.

10. Cut into wedges and serve.

Chocolate Orange Cheesecake

INGREDIENT	FOR 6-INCH CAKE	FOR 9-INCH CAKE
Fat-free cream cheese, softened	3 8-ounce packages	6 8-ounce packages
Sugar	¾ cup	1½ cups
Fat-free egg substitute	4 ounces	8 ounces
Nonfat powdered milk	¼ cup mixed with 2 tablespoons water	½ cup mixed with ¼ cup water
Fat-free sour cream	¼ cup	½ cup
Fat-free margarine, melted	¼ cup	½ cup
European-style cocoa	½ cup	1 cup
All-purpose flour	¼ cup	½ cup
Fresh lemon juice	1 tablespoon	2 tablespoons
Vanilla extract	1 teaspoon	2 teaspoons
Orange extract	1 teaspoon	2 teaspoons
Grated orange zest	1 tablespoon	2 tablespoons

CRUST

Chocolate Graham Cracker (page 10)	single recipe	double recipe

GARNISH

Low-fat whipped topping	1 cup	2 cups
European-style cocoa	1 teaspoon	2 teaspoons
Grated orange zest	1 tablespoon	2 tablespoons

Baking time	45–60 minutes	1¼–1½ hours
Serves	8	16
Calories per serving	238 (20 from fat)	238 (20 from fat)
Fat per serving	2.2 grams	2.2 grams

This creamy cheesecake blends rich chocolate with a hint of orange.

---

1. Preheat the oven to 350°F.

2. Gently pat the prepared crust mixture on the bottom and partially up the sides of a greased springform pan. Place in the freezer for 10 minutes.

3. Blend the cream cheese and sugar in an electric mixing bowl or food processor. Add the egg substitute and blend well.

4. Add the powdered milk mixture, sour cream, margarine, cocoa, and flour, mixing until the batter is smooth and well-combined. Stir in the lemon juice, vanilla and orange extracts, and orange zest by hand.

5. Remove the springform pan from the freezer. Pour the batter into the pan and smooth with a rubber spatula.

6. Place the pan on the center rack of the oven and bake until the cheesecake sets and is lightly brown. If the cake begins to brown too quickly, cover the top loosely with aluminum foil. The cheesecake is done when the center of the cake is firm to the touch.

7. Remove the cake from the oven and place on a wire rack until completely cool (about 2 hours). Once cool, refrigerate for at least 2 hours. When chilled, the cheesecake will come out of the pan easily.

8. Before removing the pan, loosen the cake from the sides with a knife or metal spatula.

9. Spoon the topping into a pastry bag and pipe it decoratively on top of the cake. Top with a dusting of cocoa and a sprinkling of orange zest.

10. Cut into wedges and serve.

Double Chocolate Mocha Cheesecake

INGREDIENT	FOR 6-INCH CAKE	FOR 9-INCH CAKE
Fat-free cream cheese, softened	3 8-ounce packages	6 8-ounce packages
Sugar	¾ cup	1½ cups
Fat-free egg substitute	4 ounces	8 ounces
Nonfat powdered milk	¼ cup mixed with 2 tablespoons water	½ cup mixed with ¼ cup water
Fat-free sour cream	¼ cup	½ cup
Fat-free margarine, melted	¼ cup	½ cup
European-style cocoa	½ cup	1 cup
Instant coffee granules	2 teaspoons	4 teaspoons
All-purpose flour	¼ cup	½ cup
Fresh lemon juice	1 tablespoon	2 tablespoons
Vanilla extract	1 teaspoon	2 teaspoons
Mini chocolate chips	¼ cup	½ cup

CRUST

Chocolate Graham Cracker (page 10)	single recipe	double recipe

GARNISH

Low-fat whipped topping	1 cup	2 cups
European-style cocoa	1 teaspoon	2 teaspoons

Baking time	45–60 minutes	1¼–1½ hours
Serves	8	16
Calories per serving	251 (27 from fat)	251 (27 from fat)
Fat per serving	3 grams	3 grams

Creamy cocoa and mini chocolate chips combine with rich coffee flavor to make this cheesecake a special treat.

---

1. Preheat the oven to 350°F.

2. Gently pat the prepared crust mixture on the bottom and partially up the sides of a greased springform pan. Place in the freezer for 10 minutes.

3. Blend the cream cheese and sugar in an electric mixing bowl or food processor. Add the egg substitute and blend well.

4. Add the powdered milk mixture, sour cream, margarine, cocoa, coffee granules, and flour, mixing until the batter is smooth and well-combined. Stir in the lemon juice and vanilla by hand. Fold in the chocolate chips.

5. Remove the springform pan from the freezer. Pour the batter into the pan and smooth with a rubber spatula.

6. Place the pan on the center rack of the oven and bake until the cheesecake sets and is lightly brown. If the cake begins to brown too quickly, cover the top loosely with aluminum foil. The cheesecake is done when the center of the cake is firm to the touch.

7. Remove the cake from the oven and place on a wire rack until completely cool (about 2 hours). Once cool, refrigerate for at least 2 hours. When chilled, the cheesecake will come out of the pan easily.

8. Before removing the pan, loosen the cake from the sides with a knife or metal spatula.

9. Spoon the topping into a pastry bag and pipe it decoratively on top of the cake. Dust with cocoa.

10. Cut into wedges and serve.

VARIATION

For a Brazilian-inspired version of this cheesecake, add 2 teaspoons of cinnamon to the filling ingredients.

White Chocolate Cheesecake

INGREDIENT	FOR 6-INCH CAKE	FOR 9-INCH CAKE
Fat-free cream cheese, softened	3 8-ounce packages	6 8-ounce packages
Sugar	¾ cup	1½ cups
Fat-free egg substitute	4 ounces	8 ounces
Nonfat powdered milk	¼ cup mixed with 2 tablespoons water	½ cup mixed with ¼ cup water
Fat-free sour cream	¼ cup	½ cup
Fat-free margarine, melted	¼ cup	½ cup
All-purpose flour	¼ cup	½ cup
Fresh lemon juice	1 tablespoon	2 tablespoons
Vanilla extract	1 teaspoon	2 teaspoons
White chocolate chips	¼ cup	½ cup
CRUST		
Chocolate Graham Cracker (page 10)	single recipe	double recipe
GARNISH		
Low-fat whipped topping	1 cup	2 cups
European-style cocoa	1 teaspoon	2 teaspoons

Baking time	45–60 minutes	1¼–1½ hours
Serves	8	16
Calories per serving	260 (18 from fat)	260 (18 from fat)
Fat per serving	2 grams	2 grams

This heavenly cheesecake is flecked with sweet white chocolate chips.

---

1. Preheat the oven to 350°F.

2. Gently pat the prepared crust mixture on the bottom and partially up the sides of a greased springform pan. Place in the freezer for 10 minutes.

3. Blend the cream cheese and sugar in an electric mixing bowl or food processor. Add the egg substitute and blend well.

4. Add the powdered milk mixture, sour cream, margarine, and flour, mixing until the batter is smooth and well-combined. Stir in the lemon juice and vanilla by hand. Fold in the white chocolate chips.

5. Remove the springform pan from the freezer. Pour the batter into the pan and smooth with a rubber spatula.

6. Place the pan on the center rack of the oven and bake until the cheesecake sets and is lightly brown. If the cake begins to brown too quickly, cover the top loosely with aluminum foil. The cheesecake is done when the center of the cake is firm to the touch.

7. Remove the cake from the oven and place on a wire rack until completely cool (about 2 hours). Once cool, refrigerate for at least 2 hours. When chilled, the cheesecake will come out of the pan easily.

8. Before removing the pan, loosen the cake from the sides with a knife or metal spatula.

9. Spoon the topping into a pastry bag and pipe it decoratively on top of the cake. Dust with cocoa.

10. Cut into wedges and serve.

Chocolate Raspberry Cheesecake

INGREDIENT	FOR 6-INCH CAKE	FOR 9-INCH CAKE
Fat-free cream cheese, softened	3 8-ounce packages	6 8-ounce packages
Sugar	¾ cup	1½ cups
Fat-free egg substitute	4 ounces	8 ounces
Nonfat powdered milk	¼ cup mixed with 2 tablespoons water	½ cup mixed with ¼ cup water
Fat-free sour cream	¼ cup	½ cup
Fat-free margarine, melted	¼ cup	½ cup
European-style cocoa	⅔ cup	1⅓ cups
All-purpose flour	¼ cup	½ cup
Raspberry extract	1 teaspoon	2 teaspoons
Vanilla extract	1 teaspoon	2 teaspoons
Fresh raspberries	½ cup	1 cup

CRUST

Chocolate Graham Cracker (page 10)	single recipe	double recipe

GARNISH

Low-fat whipped topping	1 cup	2 cups
Fresh raspberries	8	16
European-style chocolate	1 teaspoon	2 teaspoons

Baking Time	45–60 minutes	1¼–1½ hours
Serves	8	16
Calories per serving	274 (23 from fat)	274 (23 from fat)
Fat per serving	2.5 grams	2.5 grams

Chocolate and raspberries are one of my favorite flavor combinations. Be sure to try this cheesecake when fresh raspberries are in season, although the frozen variety will do in a pinch.

---

1. Preheat the oven to 350°F.

2. Gently pat the prepared crust mixture on the bottom and partially up the sides of a greased springform pan. Place in the freezer for 10 minutes.

3. Blend the cream cheese and sugar in an electric mixing bowl or food processor. Add the egg substitute and blend well.

4. Add the powdered milk mixture, sour cream, margarine, cocoa, and flour, mixing until the batter is smooth and well-combined. Stir in the raspberry and vanilla extracts by hand. Fold in the raspberries.

5. Remove the springform pan from the freezer. Pour the batter into the pan and smooth with a rubber spatula.

6. Place the pan on the center rack of the oven and bake until the cheesecake sets and is lightly brown. If the cake begins to brown too quickly, cover the top loosely with aluminum foil. The cheesecake is done when the center of the cake is firm to the touch.

7. Remove the cake from the oven and place on a wire rack until completely cool (about 2 hours). Once cool, refrigerate for at least 2 hours. When chilled, the cheesecake will come out of the pan easily.

8. Before removing the pan, loosen the cake from the sides with a knife or metal spatula.

9. Spoon the topping into a pastry bag and pipe rosettes along the edge of the cake. Place a raspberry on top of each rosette and dust with cocoa.

10. Cut into wedges and serve.

Peanut Butter and Chocolate Cheesecake

INGREDIENT	FOR 6-INCH CAKE	FOR 9-INCH CAKE
Fat-free cream cheese, softened	3 8-ounce packages	6 8-ounce packages
Sugar	¾ cup	1½ cups
Fat-free egg substitute	4 ounces	8 ounces
Nonfat powdered milk	¼ cup mixed with 2 tablespoons water	½ cup mixed with ¼ cup water
Fat-free sour cream	¼ cup	½ cup
Fat-free margarine, melted	¼ cup	½ cup
Reduced-fat peanut butter, softened	½ cup	1 cup
European-style cocoa	½ cup	1 cup
All-purpose flour	¼ cup	½ cup
Vanilla extract	1 teaspoon	2 teaspoons

CRUST

Chocolate Graham Cracker (page 10)	single recipe	double recipe

GARNISH

Low-fat whipped topping	1 cup	2 cups
Chopped, unsalted peanuts	¼ cup	½ cup

Baking Time	45–60 minutes	1¼–1½ hours
Serves	8	16
Calories per serving	340 (72 from fat)	340 (72 from fat)
Fat per serving	8 grams	8 grams

Peanut butter fans, beware! This luscious cheesecake can be habit-forming. I know its fat content may be a bit higher than the other cheesecakes in this book, but I have left it in for those special occasions when you feel the need to splurge.

---

1. Preheat the oven to 350°F.

2. Gently pat the prepared crust mixture on the bottom and partially up the sides of a greased springform pan. Place in the freezer for 10 minutes.

3. Blend the cream cheese and sugar in an electric mixing bowl or food processor. Add the egg substitute and blend well.

4. Add the powdered milk mixture, sour cream, margarine, peanut butter, cocoa, and flour, mixing until the batter is smooth and well-combined. Stir in the vanilla by hand.

5. Remove the springform pan from the freezer. Pour the batter into the pan and smooth with a rubber spatula.

6. Place the pan on the center rack of the oven and bake until the cheesecake sets and is lightly brown. If the cake begins to brown too quickly, cover the top loosely with aluminum foil. The cheesecake is done when the center of the cake is firm to the touch.

7. Remove the cake from the oven and place on a wire rack until completely cool (about 2 hours). Once cool, refrigerate for at least 2 hours. When chilled, the cheesecake will come out of the pan easily.

8. Before removing the pan, loosen the cake from the sides with a knife or metal spatula.

9. Spoon the topping into a pastry bag and pipe it decoratively on top of the cake. Sprinkle with peanuts.

10. Cut into wedges and serve.

6.

Spirited Flavors

Some of the most interesting cheesecakes are flavored with liqueurs. Cordials such as almond-flavored amaretto and licorice-flavored anisette can transform the simplest, most basic cheesecake into a uniquely exquisite dessert.

The vast number of liqueurs on the market provide limitless possibilities for cheesecake flavors. I have merely touched the tip of the iceberg by providing such "spirited" cheesecakes as Grand Marnier (page 100), Irish Cream (page 102), and Crème de Menthe (page 116). Enjoy the recipes provided in this chapter or feel free to create your own with your personal favorite liqueur.

Melon Cooler Cheesecake

INGREDIENT	FOR 6-INCH CAKE	FOR 9-INCH CAKE
Fat-free cream cheese, softened	3 8-ounce packages	6 8-ounce packages
Sugar	¾ cup	1½ cups
Fat-free egg substitute	4 ounces	8 ounces
Nonfat powdered milk	¼ cup mixed with 2 tablespoons water	½ cup mixed with ¼ cup water
Fat-free sour cream	¼ cup	½ cup
Fat-free margarine, melted	¼ cup	½ cup
All-purpose flour	¼ cup	½ cup
Melon liqueur	¼ cup	½ cup
Fresh lemon juice	⅓ cup	⅔ cup
CRUST		
Graham Cracker (page 8)	single recipe	double recipe
GARNISH		
Low-fat whipped topping	1 cup	2 cups
Thin honeydew wedges	8 (¼ honeydew)	16 (½ honeydew)
Kiwi, peeled and sliced	1	1

Baking Time	45–60 minutes	1¼–1½ hours
Serves	8	16
Calories per serving	302 (9 from fat)	302 (9 from fat)
Fat per serving	1 gram	1 gram

What can enhance with the cool tang of honeydew melon? The rich creaminess of cheesecake, of course!

---

1. Preheat the oven to 350°F.

2. Gently pat the prepared crust mixture on the bottom and partially up the sides of a greased springform pan. Place in the freezer for 10 minutes.

3. Blend the cream cheese and sugar in an electric mixing bowl or food processor. Add the egg substitute and blend well.

4. Add the powdered milk mixture, sour cream, margarine, and flour, mixing until the batter is smooth and well-combined. Stir in the liqueur and lemon juice by hand.

5. Remove the springform pan from the freezer. Pour the batter into the pan and smooth with a rubber spatula.

6. Place the pan on the center rack of the oven and bake until the cheesecake sets and is lightly brown. If the cake begins to brown too quickly, cover the top loosely with aluminum foil. The cheesecake is done when the center of the cake is firm to the touch.

7. Remove the cake from the oven and place on a wire rack until completely cool (about 2 hours). Once cool, refrigerate the cake for at least 2 hours. When chilled, the cheesecake will come out of the pan easily.

8. Before removing the pan, loosen the cake from the sides with a knife or metal spatula.

9. Spoon the topping into a pastry bag and pipe rosettes along the top edge of the cake. Place a slice of honeydew melon between the rosettes, and arrange the kiwi slices in the center.

10. Cut into wedges and serve.

Passion Fruit Cheesecake

INGREDIENT	FOR 6-INCH CAKE	FOR 9-INCH CAKE
Fat-free cream cheese, softened	3 8-ounce packages	6 8-ounce packages
Sugar	¾ cup	1½ cups
Fat-free egg substitute	4 ounces	8 ounces
Nonfat powdered milk	¼ cup mixed with 2 tablespoons water	½ cup mixed with ¼ cup water
Fat-free sour cream	¼ cup	½ cup
Fat-free margarine, melted	¼ cup	½ cup
All-purpose flour	¼ cup	½ cup
Passion fruit liqueur	¼ cup	½ cup
Fresh lemon juice	⅓ cup	⅔ cup

CRUST

Coconut Graham Cracker (page 20)	single recipe	double recipe

GARNISH

Low-fat whipped topping	1 cup	2 cups
Thin mango wedges	8 (½ mango)	16 (1 mango)
Kiwi, peeled and sliced	1	1

Baking Time	45–60 minutes	1¼–1½ hours
Serves	8	16
Calories per serving	314 (9 from fat)	314 (9 from fat)
Fat per serving	1 gram	1 gram

Tropical fruit flavors characterize this special-occasion cheesecake.

---

1. Preheat the oven to 350°F.

2. Gently pat the prepared crust mixture on the bottom and partially up the sides of a greased springform pan. Place in the freezer for 10 minutes.

3. Blend the cream cheese and sugar in an electric mixing bowl or food processor. Add the egg substitute and blend well.

4. Add the powdered milk mixture, sour cream, margarine, and flour, mixing until the batter is smooth and well-combined. Stir in the liqueur and lemon juice by hand.

5. Remove the springform pan from the freezer. Pour the batter into the pan and smooth with a rubber spatula.

6. Place the pan on the center rack of the oven and bake until the cheesecake sets and is lightly brown. If the cake begins to brown too quickly, cover the top loosely with aluminum foil. The cheesecake is done when the center of the cake is firm to the touch.

7. Remove the cake from the oven and place on a wire rack until completely cool (about 2 hours). Once cool, refrigerate the cake for at least 2 hours. When chilled, the cheesecake will come out of the pan easily.

8. Before removing the pan, loosen the cake from the sides with a knife or metal spatula.

9. Spoon the topping into a pastry bag and pipe rosettes along the top edge of the cake. Place a slice of mango between the rosettes, and arrange the kiwi slices in the center.

10. Cut into wedges and serve.

Grand Marnier Cheesecake

INGREDIENT	FOR 6-INCH CAKE	FOR 9-INCH CAKE
Fat-free cream cheese, softened	2 8-ounce packages	4 8-ounce packages
Firm tofu, mashed	8 ounces	16 ounces
Sugar	¾ cup	1½ cups
Fat-free egg substitute	4 ounces	8 ounces
Nonfat powdered milk	¼ cup mixed with 2 tablespoons water	½ cup mixed with ¼ cup water
Fat-free sour cream	¼ cup	½ cup
Fat-free yogurt	¼ cup	½ cup
Grand Marnier liqueur	¼ cup	½ cup
Grated orange zest	2 tablespoons	¼ cup

CRUST

Zesty Orange Graham Cracker (page 12)	single recipe	double recipe

GARNISH

Low-fat whipped topping	1 cup	2 cups
Grated orange zest	1 tablespoon	2 tablespoons

Baking Time	45–60 minutes	1¼–1½ hours
Serves	8	16
Calories per serving	316 (24 from fat)	316 (24 from fat)
Fat per serving	2.75 grams	2.75 grams

Grand Marnier's sweet orange tang really shines in this luscious cheesecake.

---

1. Preheat the oven to 350°F.

2. Gently pat the prepared crust mixture on the bottom and partially up the sides of a greased springform pan. Place in the freezer for 10 minutes.

3. Blend the cream cheese, tofu, and sugar in an electric mixer or food processor. Add the egg substitute and blend well.

4. Add the powdered milk mixture, sour cream, and yogurt, mixing until the batter is smooth and well-combined. Stir in the Grand Marnier and orange zest by hand.

5. Remove the springform pan from the freezer. Pour the batter into the pan and smooth with a rubber spatula.

6. Place the pan on the center rack of the oven and bake until the cheesecake sets and is lightly brown. If the cake begins to brown too quickly, cover the top loosely with aluminum foil. The cheesecake is done when the center of the cake is firm to the touch.

7. Remove the cake from the oven and place on a wire rack until completely cool (about 2 hours). Once cool, refrigerate for at least 2 hours. When chilled, the cheesecake will come out of the pan easily.

8. Before removing the pan, loosen the cake from the sides with a knife or metal spatula.

9. Spoon the whipped topping decoratively on top of the cake and sprinkle with orange zest.

10. Cut into wedges and serve.

Irish Cream Cheesecake

INGREDIENT	FOR 6-INCH CAKE	FOR 9-INCH CAKE
Fat-free cream cheese, softened	2 8-ounce packages	4 8-ounce packages
Firm tofu, mashed	8 ounces	16 ounces
Sugar	¾ cup	1½ cups
Fat-free egg substitute	4 ounces	8 ounces
Nonfat powdered milk	¼ cup mixed with 2 tablespoons water	½ cup mixed with ¼ cup water
Fat-free sour cream	¼ cup	½ cup
Fat-free yogurt	¼ cup	½ cup
Light Irish Cream	⅓ cup	⅔ cup
CRUST		
Graham Cracker (page 8)	single recipe	double recipe
GARNISH		
Low-fat whipped topping	1 cup	2 cups
European-style cocoa	1 teaspoon	2 teaspoons

Baking Time	45–60 minutes	1¼–1½ hours
Serves	8	16
Calories per serving	270 (35 from fat)	270 (35 from fat)
Fat per serving	3.85 grams	3.85 grams

Although this rich, creamy cheesecake may be the perfect St. Patrick's Day treat, feel free to enjoy it any time.

1. Preheat the oven to 350°F.

2. Gently pat the prepared crust mixture on the bottom and partially up the sides of a greased springform pan. Place in the freezer for 10 minutes.

3. Blend the cream cheese, tofu, and sugar in an electric mixer or food processor. Add the egg substitute and blend well.

4. Add the powdered milk mixture, sour cream, and yogurt, mixing until the batter is smooth and well-combined. Stir in the Irish Cream by hand.

5. Remove the springform pan from the freezer. Pour the batter into the pan and smooth with a rubber spatula.

6. Place the pan on the center rack of the oven and bake until the cheesecake sets and is lightly brown. If the cake begins to brown too quickly, cover the top loosely with aluminum foil. The cheesecake is done when the center of the cake is firm to the touch.

7. Remove the cake from the oven and place on a wire rack until completely cool (about 2 hours). Once cool, refrigerate for at least 2 hours. When chilled, the cheesecake will come out of the pan easily.

8. Before removing the pan, loosen the cake from the sides with a knife or metal spatula.

9. Spoon the whipped topping decoratively on top of the cake and top with a sprinkling of cocoa.

10. Cut into wedges and serve.

Parfait Amour Cheesecake

INGREDIENT	FOR 6-INCH CAKE	FOR 9-INCH CAKE
Fat-free cream cheese, softened	2 8-ounce packages	4 8-ounce packages
Firm tofu, mashed	8 ounces	16 ounces
Sugar	¾ cup	1½ cups
Fat-free egg substitute	4 ounces	8 ounces
Nonfat powdered milk	¼ cup mixed with 2 tablespoons water	½ cup mixed with ¼ cup water
Fat-free sour cream	¼ cup	½ cup
Fat-free yogurt	¼ cup	½ cup
Parfait Amour	½ cup	1 cup
CRUST		
Graham Cracker (page 8)	single recipe	double recipe
GARNISH		
Low-fat whipped topping	1 cup	2 cups

Baking Time	45–60 minutes	1¼–1½ hours
Serves	8	16
Calories per serving	311 (24 from fat)	311 (24 from fat)
Fat per serving	2.75 grams	2.75 grams

The perfect ending to a romantic dinner.

---

1. Preheat the oven to 350°F.

2. Gently pat the prepared crust mixture on the bottom and partially up the sides of a greased springform pan. Place in the freezer for 10 minutes.

3. Blend the cream cheese, tofu, and sugar in an electric mixer or food processor. Add the egg substitute and blend well.

4. Add the powdered milk mixture, sour cream, and yogurt, mixing until the batter is smooth and well-combined. Stir in the Parfait Amour by hand.

5. Remove the springform pan from the freezer. Pour the batter into the pan and smooth with a rubber spatula.

6. Place the pan on the center rack of the oven and bake until the cheesecake sets and is lightly brown. If the cake begins to brown too quickly, cover the top loosely with aluminum foil. The cheesecake is done when the center of the cake is firm to the touch.

7. Remove the cake from the oven and place on a wire rack until completely cool (about 2 hours). Once cool, refrigerate for at least 2 hours. When chilled, the cheesecake will come out of the pan easily.

8. Before removing the pan, loosen the cake from the sides with a knife or metal spatula.

9. Garnish with whipped topping and fresh roses.

10. Cut into wedges and serve.

Heavenly Hazelnut Cheesecake

INGREDIENT	FOR 6-INCH CAKE	FOR 9-INCH CAKE
Fat-free cream cheese, softened	3 8-ounce packages	6 8-ounce packages
Sugar	¾ cup	1½ cups
Fat-free egg substitute	4 ounces	8 ounces
Nonfat powdered milk	¼ cup mixed with 2 tablespoons water	½ cup mixed with ¼ cup water
Fat-free sour cream	¼ cup	½ cup
Fat-free margarine, melted	¼ cup	½ cup
All-purpose flour	¼ cup	½ cup
Hazelnut liqueur	¼ cup	½ cup
Vanilla extract	1 teaspoon	2 teaspoons

CRUST

Graham Cracker (page 8)	single recipe	double recipe

GARNISH

Low-fat whipped topping	1 cup	2 cups
Chocolate-dipped hazelnuts (page 114)	8	16

Baking Time	45–60 minutes	1¼–1½ hours
Serves	8	16
Calories per serving	345 (24 from fat)	345 (24 from fat)
Fat per serving	2.7 grams	2.7 grams

This cheesecake is a hazelnut lover's dream.

---

1. Preheat the oven to 350°F.

2. Gently pat the prepared crust mixture on the bottom and partially up the sides of a greased springform pan. Place in the freezer for 10 minutes.

3. Blend the cream cheese and sugar in an electric mixing bowl or food processor. Add the egg substitute and blend well.

4. Add the powdered milk mixture, sour cream, margarine, and flour, mixing until the batter is smooth and well-combined. Stir in the liqueur and vanilla by hand.

5. Remove the springform pan from the freezer. Pour the batter into the pan and smooth with a rubber spatula.

6. Place the pan on the center rack of the oven and bake until the cheesecake sets and is lightly brown. If the cake begins to brown too quickly, cover the top loosely with aluminum foil. The cheesecake is done when the center of the cake is firm to the touch.

7. Remove the cake from the oven and place on a wire rack until completely cool (about 2 hours). Once cool, refrigerate for at least 2 hours. When chilled, the cheesecake will come out of the pan easily.

8. Before removing the pan, loosen the cake from the sides with a knife or metal spatula.

9. Spoon the topping into a pastry bag and pipe rosettes along the top edge of the cake. Place a chocolate-dipped hazelnut on each rosette.

10. Cut into wedges and serve.

Amaretto Cheesecake

INGREDIENT	FOR 6-INCH CAKE	FOR 9-INCH CAKE
Fat-free cream cheese, softened	3 8-ounce packages	6 8-ounce packages
Sugar	¾ cup	1½ cups
Fat-free egg substitute	4 ounces	8 ounces
Nonfat powdered milk	¼ cup mixed with 2 tablespoons water	½ cup mixed with ¼ cup water
Fat-free sour cream	¼ cup	½ cup
Fat-free margarine, melted	¼ cup	½ cup
All-purpose flour	¼ cup	½ cup
Amaretto liqueur	¼ cup	½ cup
Vanilla extract	1 teaspoon	2 teaspoons
CRUST		
Graham Cracker (page 8)	single recipe	double recipe
GARNISH		
Low-fat whipped topping	1 cup	2 cups
Slivered almonds	1 teaspoon	2 teaspoons

Baking Time	45–60 minutes	1¼–1½ hours
Serves	8	16
Calories per serving	317 (7 from fat)	317 (7 from fat)
Fat per serving	0.8 gram	0.8 gram

This amaretto cheesecake with its delicate almond flavor is really special.

1. Preheat the oven to 350°F.

2. Gently pat the prepared crust mixture on the bottom and partially up the sides of a greased springform pan. Place in the freezer for 10 minutes.

3. Blend the cream cheese and sugar in an electric mixing bowl or food processor. Add the egg substitute and blend well.

4. Add the powdered milk mixture, sour cream, margarine, and flour, mixing until the batter is smooth and well-combined. Stir in the amaretto and vanilla by hand.

5. Remove the springform pan from the freezer. Pour the batter into the pan and smooth with a rubber spatula.

6. Place the pan on the center rack of the oven and bake until the cheesecake sets and is lightly brown. If the cake begins to brown too quickly, cover the top loosely with aluminum foil. The cheesecake is done when the center of the cake is firm to the touch.

7. Remove the cake from the oven and place on a wire rack until completely cool (about 2 hours). Once cool, refrigerate for at least 2 hours. When chilled, the cheesecake will come out of the pan easily.

8. Before removing the pan, loosen the cake from the sides with a knife or metal spatula.

9. Spoon the topping decoratively on the cake and top with a sprinkling of slivered almonds.

10. Cut into wedges and serve.

Anisette Cheesecake

INGREDIENT	FOR 6-INCH CAKE	FOR 9-INCH CAKE
Fat-free cream cheese, softened	3 8-ounce packages	6 8-ounce packages
Sugar	¾ cup	1½ cups
Fat-free egg substitute	4 ounces	8 ounces
Nonfat powdered milk	¼ cup mixed with 2 tablespoons water	½ cup mixed with ¼ cup water
Fat-free sour cream	¼ cup	½ cup
Fat-free margarine, melted	¼ cup	½ cup
All-purpose flour	¼ cup	½ cup
Anisette liqueur	¼ cup	½ cup
Vanilla extract	1 teaspoon	2 teaspoons

CRUST

Graham Cracker (page 8)	single recipe	double recipe

GARNISH

Low-fat whipped topping	1 cup	2 cups
Mini licorice jelly beans	8	16

Baking Time	45–60 minutes	1¼ –1½ hours
Serves	8	16
Calories per serving	313 (9 from fat)	313 (9 from fat)
Fat per serving	1 gram	1 gram

If you like licorice, you'll love this cheesecake.

---

1. Preheat the oven to 350°F.

2. Gently pat the prepared crust mixture on the bottom and partially up the sides of a greased springform pan. Place in the freezer for 10 minutes.

3. Blend the cream cheese and sugar in an electric mixing bowl or food processor. Add the egg substitute and blend well.

4. Add the powdered milk mixture, sour cream, margarine, and flour, mixing until the batter is smooth and well-combined. Stir in the anisette and vanilla by hand.

5. Remove the springform pan from the freezer. Pour the batter into the pan and smooth with a rubber spatula.

6. Place the pan on the center rack of the oven and bake until the cheesecake sets and is lightly brown. If the cake begins to brown too quickly, cover the top loosely with aluminum foil. The cheesecake is done when the center of the cake is firm to the touch.

7. Remove the cake from the oven and place on a wire rack until completely cool (about 2 hours). Once cool, refrigerate for at least 2 hours. When chilled, the cheesecake will come out of the pan easily.

8. Before removing the pan, loosen the cake from the sides with a knife or metal spatula.

9. Spoon the topping into a pastry bag and pipe rosettes along the top edge of the cake. Place a jelly bean on each rosette.

10. Cut into wedges and serve.

Creamy Kahlua Cheesecake

INGREDIENT	FOR 6-INCH CAKE	FOR 9-INCH CAKE
Fat-free ricotta cheese	16 ounces	32 ounces
Sugar	¾ cup	1½ cups
Fat-free egg substitute	8 ounces	16 ounces
Nonfat powdered milk	¼ cup mixed with 2 tablespoons water	½ cup mixed with ¼ cup water
Fat-free sour cream	½ cup	1 cup
Fat-free margarine, melted	¼ cup	½ cup
All-purpose flour	¼ cup	½ cup
Kahlua	¼ cup	½ cup
Vanilla extract	1 teaspoon	2 teaspoons

CRUST

Graham Cracker (page 8)	single recipe	double recipe

GARNISH

Low-fat whipped topping	1 cup	2 cups
Chocolate-coated coffee beans (page 115)	¼ cup	½ cup

Baking Time	45–60 minutes	1¼–1½ hours
Serves	8	16
Calories per serving	349 (9 from fat)	349 (9 from fat)
Fat per serving	1 gram	1 gram

Kahlua's classic coffee flavor does wonders for this special-occasion cheesecake.

---

1. Preheat the oven to 350°F.

2. Gently pat the prepared crust mixture on the bottom and partially up the sides of a greased springform pan. Place in the freezer for 10 minutes.

3. Blend the ricotta cheese and sugar in an electric mixing bowl or food processor. Add the egg substitute and blend well.

4. Add the powdered milk mixture, sour cream, margarine, and flour, mixing until the batter is smooth and well-combined. Stir in the kahlua and vanilla by hand.

5. Remove the springform pan from the freezer. Pour the batter into the pan and smooth with a rubber spatula.

6. Place the pan on the center rack of the oven and bake until the cheesecake sets and is lightly brown. If the cake begins to brown too quickly, cover the top loosely with aluminum foil. The cheesecake is done when the center of the cake is firm to the touch.

7. Remove the cake from the oven and place on a wire rack until completely cool (about 2 hours). Once cool, refrigerate for at least 2 hours. When chilled, the cheesecake will come out of the pan easily.

8. Before removing the pan, loosen the cake from the sides with a knife or metal spatula.

9. Spoon the topping into a pastry bag and pipe it decoratively on top of the cake. Scatter the coffee beans on top.

10. Cut into wedges and serve.

Chocolate-Dipped Hazelnuts

Crunchy hazelnuts that have been dipped in silky chocolate can serve as the perfect garnish for a number of cheesecakes, including the Heavenly Hazelnut (page 106) and the No-Bake Chocolate Hazelnut (page 280).

¼ cup hazelnuts
1 ounce milk or dark chocolate

1. Melt the chocolate in a double boiler, stirring until it is completely melted and smooth.

2. Carefully dip the bottom half of each hazelnut in the chocolate and place on a wax paper-lined cookie sheet.

3. Refrigerate for 30 minutes to allow the chocolate to harden.

Chocolate-Coated
Coffee Beans

Want to add a tasty, attractive touch to such coffee-flavored cheesecakes as Creamy Kahlua (page 112) and Café au Lait (page 182)? Simply toss a handful of chocolate-coated coffee beans on top of the cake before serving.

¼ cup coffee beans
1 ounce milk or dark chocolate

1. Melt the chocolate in a double boiler, stirring until it is completely melted and smooth.

2. Toss the coffee beans in the chocolate and stir to coat.

3. Using a fork, remove the beans and place them on a wax paper-lined cookie sheet.

4. Refrigerate for 30 minutes to allow the chocolate to harden.

Crème de Menthe Cheesecake

INGREDIENT	FOR 6-INCH CAKE	FOR 9-INCH CAKE
Fat-free cream cheese, softened	3 8-ounce packages	6 8-ounce packages
Sugar	¾ cup	1½ cups
Fat-free egg substitute	4 ounces	8 ounces
Nonfat powdered milk	¼ cup mixed with 2 tablespoons water	½ cup mixed with ¼ cup water
Fat-free sour cream	¼ cup	½ cup
Fat-free margarine, melted	¼ cup	½ cup
All-purpose flour	¼ cup	½ cup
Crème de menthe liqueur	¼ cup	½ cup
Vanilla extract	1 teaspoon	2 teaspoons

CRUST

Chocolate Graham Cracker (page 10)	single recipe	double recipe

GARNISH

Low-fat whipped topping	1 cup	2 cups
Mint leaves	8	16

Baking Time	45–60 minutes	1¼–1½ hours
Serves	8	16
Calories per serving	307 (9 from fat)	307 (9 from fat)
Fat per serving	1 gram	1 gram

Try this cheesecake when you're in the mood for something cool and minty.

---

1. Preheat the oven to 350°F.

2. Gently pat the prepared crust mixture on the bottom and partially up the sides of a greased springform pan. Place in the freezer for 10 minutes.

3. Blend the cream cheese and sugar in an electric mixing bowl or food processor. Add the egg substitute and blend well.

4. Add the powdered milk mixture, sour cream, margarine, and flour, mixing until the batter is smooth and well-combined. Stir in the crème de menthe and vanilla by hand.

5. Remove the springform pan from the freezer. Pour the batter into the pan and smooth with a rubber spatula.

6. Place the pan on the center rack of the oven and bake until the cheesecake sets and is lightly brown. If the cake begins to brown too quickly, cover the top loosely with aluminum foil. The cheesecake is done when the center of the cake is firm to the touch.

7. Remove the cake from the oven and place on a wire rack until completely cool (about 2 hours). Once cool, refrigerate for at least 2 hours. When chilled, the cheesecake will come out of the pan easily.

8. Before removing the pan, loosen the cake from the sides with a knife or metal spatula.

9. Spoon the whipped topping into a pastry bag and pipe rosettes in a circle on top of the cake. Place a mint sprig under each rosette, with the leaves facing toward the outer edge.

10. Cut into wedges and serve.

Grasshopper Cheesecake

INGREDIENT	FOR 6-INCH CAKE	FOR 9-INCH CAKE
Fat-free cream cheese, softened	3 8-ounce packages	6 8-ounce packages
Sugar	¾ cup	1½ cups
Fat-free egg substitute	4 ounces	8 ounces
Nonfat powdered milk	¼ cup mixed with 2 tablespoons water	½ cup mixed with ¼ cup water
Fat-free sour cream	¼ cup	½ cup
Fat-free margarine, melted	¼ cup	½ cup
All-purpose flour	¼ cup	½ cup
Crème de menthe liqueur	⅛ cup	¼ cup
Crème de cacao liqueur	⅛ cup	⅛ cup
Vanilla extract	1 teaspoon	2 teaspoons

CRUST

Chocolate Graham Cracker (page 10)	single recipe	double recipe

GARNISH

Low-fat whipped topping	1 cup	2 cups
European-style cocoa	1 teaspoon	2 teaspoons

Baking Time	45–60 minutes	1¼–1½ hours
Serves	8	16
Calories per serving	307 (9 from fat)	307 (9 from fat)
Fat per serving	1 gram	1 gram

The combination of crème de menthe and crème de cacao makes for a very special dessert.

---

1. Preheat the oven to 350°F.

2. Gently pat the prepared crust mixture on the bottom and partially up the sides of a greased springform pan. Place in the freezer for 10 minutes.

3. Blend the cream cheese and sugar in an electric mixing bowl or food processor. Add the egg substitute and blend well.

4. Add the powdered milk mixture, sour cream, margarine, and flour, mixing until the batter is smooth and well-combined. Stir in the crème de menthe, crème de cacao, and vanilla by hand.

5. Remove the springform pan from the freezer. Pour the batter into the pan and smooth with a rubber spatula.

6. Place the pan on the center rack of the oven and bake until the cheesecake sets and is lightly brown. If the cake begins to brown too quickly, cover the top loosely with aluminum foil. The cheesecake is done when the center of the cake is firm to the touch.

7. Remove the cake from the oven and place on a wire rack until completely cool (about 2 hours). Once cool, refrigerate for at least 2 hours. When chilled, the cheesecake will come out of the pan easily.

8. Before removing the pan, loosen the cake from the sides with a knife or metal spatula.

9. Spoon the whipped topping into a pastry bag and pipe it decoratively on top of the cake. Dust with cocoa.

10. Cut into wedges and serve.

Cassis Cheesecake

INGREDIENT	FOR 6-INCH CAKE	FOR 9-INCH CAKE
Fat-free cream cheese, softened	3 8-ounce packages	6 8-ounce packages
Sugar	¾ cup	1½ cups
Fat-free egg substitute	4 ounces	8 ounces
Nonfat powdered milk	¼ cup mixed with 2 tablespoons water	½ cup mixed with ¼ cup water
Fat-free sour cream	¼ cup	½ cup
Fat-free margarine, melted	¼ cup	½ cup
All-purpose flour	¼ cup	½ cup
Cassis liqueur	¼ cup	½ cup
Vanilla extract	1 teaspoon	2 teaspoons

CRUST

Graham Cracker (page 8)	single recipe	double recipe

GARNISH

Low-fat whipped topping	1 cup	2 cups
Fresh or candied violets (page 124)	8	16

Baking Time	45–60 minutes	1¼–1½ hours
Serves	8	16
Calories per serving	296 (9 from fat)	296 (9 from fat)
Fat per serving	1 gram	1 gram

Cassis, a liqueur made from black currants, is one of my favorites. It's a sensational cheesecake flavor.

---

1. Preheat the oven to 350°F.

2. Gently pat the prepared crust mixture on the bottom and partially up the sides of a greased springform pan. Place in the freezer for 10 minutes.

3. Blend the cream cheese and sugar in an electric mixing bowl or food processor. Add the egg substitute and blend well.

4. Add the powdered milk mixture, sour cream, margarine, and flour, mixing until the batter is smooth and well-combined. Stir in the cassis and vanilla by hand.

5. Remove the springform pan from the freezer. Pour the batter into the pan and smooth with a rubber spatula.

6. Place the pan on the center rack of the oven and bake until the cheesecake sets and is lightly brown. If the cake begins to brown too quickly, cover the top loosely with aluminum foil. The cheesecake is done when the center of the cake is firm to the touch.

7. Remove the cake from the oven and place on a wire rack until completely cool (about 2 hours). Once cool, refrigerate for at least 2 hours. When chilled, the cheesecake will come out of the pan easily.

8. Before removing the pan, loosen the cake from the sides with a knife or metal spatula.

9. Spoon the topping into a pastry bag and pipe rosettes along the top edge of the cake. Place a violet on each rosette.

10. Cut into wedges and serve.

Mixed Tropical Fruit Cheesecake

INGREDIENT	FOR 6-INCH CAKE	FOR 9-INCH CAKE
Fat-free cream cheese, softened	3 8-ounce packages	6 8-ounce packages
Sugar	¾ cup	1½ cups
Fat-free egg substitute	4 ounces	8 ounces
Nonfat powdered milk	¼ cup mixed with 2 tablespoons water	½ cup mixed with ¼ cup water
Fat-free sour cream	¼ cup	½ cup
Fat-free margarine, melted	¼ cup	½ cup
Mixed tropical fruit yogurt	3 ounces	6 ounces
All-purpose flour	¼ cup	½ cup
Tropical fruit liqueur	¼ cup	½ cup
Vanilla extract	1 teaspoon	2 teaspoons

CRUST

Coconut Graham Cracker (page 20)	single recipe	double recipe

GARNISH

Low-fat whipped topping	1 cup	2 cups
Mango, peeled and sliced	⅓ cup	⅔ cup
Papaya, peeled and sliced	⅓ cup	⅔ cup
Kiwi, peeled and sliced	1	1

Baking Time	45–60 minutes	1¼–1½ hours
Serves	8	16
Calories per serving	329 (9 from fat)	329 (9 from fat)
Fat per serving	1 gram	1 gram

Although I've presented a number of different tropical fruit flavored cheesecakes, this "spirited" version is truly unique.

1. Preheat the oven to 350°F.

2. Gently pat the prepared crust mixture on the bottom and partially up the sides of a greased springform pan. Place in the freezer for 10 minutes.

3. Blend the cream cheese and sugar in an electric mixing bowl or food processor. Add the egg substitute and blend well.

4. Add the powdered milk mixture, sour cream, margarine, and flour, mixing until the batter is smooth and well-combined. Stir in the liqueur and vanilla by hand.

5. Remove the springform pan from the freezer. Pour the batter into the pan and smooth with a rubber spatula.

6. Place the pan on the center rack of the oven and bake until the cheesecake sets and is lightly brown. If the cake begins to brown too quickly, cover the top loosely with aluminum foil. The cheesecake is done when the center of the cake is firm to the touch.

7. Remove the cake from the oven and place on a wire rack until completely cool (about 2 hours). Once cool, refrigerate for at least 2 hours. When chilled, the cheesecake will come out of the pan easily.

8. Before removing the pan, loosen the cake from the sides with a knife or metal spatula.

9. Spoon the topping into a pastry bag and pipe rosettes along the top edge of the cake. Place slices of mango and papaya between the rosettes, and arrange the kiwi slices in the center.

10. Cut into wedges and serve.

Making Candied Violets

Edible candied violets, which are beautiful for decorating a number of cheesecake creations, are simple and easy to make. They are the perfect crown for the Cassis Cheesecake found on page 120.

8 fresh violets or violas
¼ cup honey
¼ cup granulated sugar or fructose

1. Bring the honey and water to boil in a small saucepan while stirring constantly. Remove from the heat and allow to cool.

2. Using a paintbrush, brush the syrup on each flower petal, then dip the flower in sugar.

3. Place on a wax paper-lined cookie sheet and allow to dry at room temperature for 1 hour.

4. Place the candied flowers in an airtight container and store in a dry place for up to one month. You can also store in the freezer up to six months.

7.

Special-Occasion Cheesecakes

This chapter was created to satisfy those times when only the most special of desserts will do. It presents cheesecakes with unique flavorings and unusual ingredients.

To grace your holiday table, choose from cheesecakes such as Sweet Sugarplum (page 126), Creamy Eggnog (page 132), and Perfect Pumpkin (page 134). Having a special dinner party? To end it on a perfect note, serve the Butterscotch Sundae Cheesecake (page 142) or the Rose Petal Cheesecake (page140). Or try the rich Baklava Cheesecake (page 148) with its crisp phyllo-dough crust—a sure-fire dessert to impress any guest.

Sweet Sugarplum Cheesecake

INGREDIENT	FOR 6-INCH CAKE	FOR 9-INCH CAKE
Fat-free cream cheese, softened	3 8-ounce packages	6 8-ounce packages
Sugar	¾ cup	1½ cups
Fat-free egg substitute	4 ounces	8 ounces
Nonfat powdered milk	¼ cup mixed with 2 tablespoons water	½ cup mixed with ¼ cup water
Fat-free sour cream	¼ cup	½ cup
Fat-free margarine, melted	¼ cup	½ cup
All-fruit plum preserves	¼ cup	½ cup
All-purpose flour	¼ cup	½ cup
Fresh lemon juice	1 tablespoon	2 tablespoons
Vanilla extract	1 teaspoon	2 teaspoons
Puréed plums, fresh or frozen*	½ cup	1 cup

CRUST

Graham Cracker (page 8)	single recipe	double recipe

GARNISH

Low-fat topping	1 cup	2 cups
Pitted plum slices	8	16

* Be sure to thaw and drain if using frozen variety.

Baking Time	45–60 minutes	1¼–1½ hours
Serves	8	16
Calories per serving	244 (9 from fat)	244 (9 from fat)
Fat per serving	1 gram	1 gram

Sweet, simple, and very special.

---

1. Preheat the oven to 350°F.

2. Gently pat the prepared crust mixture on the bottom and partially up the sides of a greased springform pan. Place in the freezer for 10 minutes.

3. Blend the cream cheese and sugar in an electric mixing bowl or food processor. Add the egg substitute and blend well.

4. Add the powdered milk mixture, sour cream, margarine, preserves, and flour, mixing until the batter is smooth and well-combined. Stir in the lemon juice and vanilla by hand. Fold in the plums.

5. Remove the springform pan from the freezer. Pour the batter into the pan and smooth with a rubber spatula.

6. Place the pan on the center rack of the oven and bake until the cheesecake sets and is lightly brown. If the cake begins to brown too quickly, cover the top loosely with aluminum foil. The cheesecake is done when the center of the cake is firm to the touch.

7. Remove the cake from the oven and place on a wire rack until completely cool (about 2 hours). Once cool, refrigerate for at least 2 hours. When chilled, the cheesecake will come out of the pan easily.

8. Before removing the pan, loosen the cake from the sides with a knife or metal spatula.

9. Spoon the whipped topping into a pastry bag and pipe it decoratively on top of the cake. Top with plum slices.

10. Cut into wedges and serve.

Tutti-Frutti Cheesecake

INGREDIENT	FOR 6-INCH CAKE	FOR 9-INCH CAKE
Fat-free cream cheese, softened	3 8-ounce packages	6 8-ounce packages
Honey	½ cup	1 cups
Fat-free egg substitute	4 ounces	8 ounces
Nonfat powdered milk	¼ cup mixed with 2 tablespoons water	½ cup mixed with ¼ cup water
Fat-free sour cream	¼ cup	½ cup
Fat-free margarine, melted	¼ cup	½ cup
All-purpose flour	¼ cup	½ cup
Fresh lemon juice	1 tablespoon	2 tablespoons
Cherry extract	½ teaspoon	1 teaspoon
Pineapple extract	½ teaspoon	1 teaspoon
Chopped dried fruit mix	1 cup	2 cups

CRUST

Coconut Oat (page 32)	single recipe	double recipe

GARNISH

Low-fat whipped topping	1 cup	2 cups
Flaked coconut	1 teaspoon	2 teaspoons
Maraschino cherries	8	16

Baking Time	45–60 minutes	1¼–1½ hours
Serves	8	16
Calories per serving	259 (48 from fat)	259 (48 from fat)
Fat per serving	5.4 grams	5.4 grams

This unique cheesecake is flecked with pieces of sweet dried fruit.

1. Preheat the oven to 350°F.

2. Gently pat the prepared crust mixture on the bottom and partially up the sides of a greased springform pan. Place in the freezer for 10 minutes.

3. Blend the cream cheese and sugar in an electric mixing bowl or food processor. Add the egg substitute and blend well.

4. Add the powdered milk mixture, sour cream, margarine, and flour, mixing until the batter is smooth and well-combined. Stir in the lemon juice, and cherry and pineapple extracts by hand. Fold in the dried fruit.

5. Remove the springform pan from the freezer. Pour the batter into the pan and smooth with a rubber spatula.

6. Place the pan on the center rack of the oven and bake until the cheesecake sets and is lightly brown. If the cake begins to brown too quickly, cover the top loosely with aluminum foil. The cheesecake is done when the center of the cake is firm to the touch.

7. Remove the cake from the oven and place on a wire rack until completely cool (about 2 hours). Once cool, refrigerate for at least 2 hours. When chilled, the cheesecake will come out of the pan easily.

8. Before removing the pan, loosen the cake from the sides with a knife or metal spatula.

9. Spoon the topping into a pastry bag and pipe it decoratively on top of the cake. Sprinkle with coconut and top with cherries.

10. Cut into wedges and serve.

Cherry-Mango Cheesecake

INGREDIENT	FOR 6-INCH CAKE	FOR 9-INCH CAKE
Fat-free cream cheese, softened	2 8-ounce packages	4 8-ounce packages
Firm tofu, mashed	8 ounces	16 ounces
Sugar	¾ cup	1½ cups
Fat-free egg substitute	4 ounces	8 ounces
Nonfat powdered milk	¼ cup mixed with 2 tablespoons water	½ cup mixed with ¼ cup water
Fat-free sour cream	¼ cup	½ cup
Fat-free yogurt	¼ cup	½ cup
Vanilla extract	1 teaspoon	2 teaspoons
Puréed mango	¼ cup	½ cup
Dark sweet cherries, pitted and halved	½ cup	1 cup
CRUST		
Chewy Oat (page 22)	single recipe	double recipe
GARNISH		
Low-fat whipped topping	1 cup	2 cups
Dark sweet pitted cherries	8	16

Baking Time	45–60 minutes	1¼–1½ hours
Serves	8	16
Calories per serving	236 (24 from fat)	236 (24 from fat)
Fat per serving	2.75 grams	2.75 grams

This unlikely combination makes a sensational cake.

---

1. Preheat the oven to 350°F.

2. Gently pat the prepared crust mixture on the bottom and partially up the sides of a greased springform pan. Place in the freezer for 10 minutes.

3. Blend the cream cheese, tofu, and sugar in an electric mixer or food processor. Add the egg substitute and blend well.

4. Add the powdered milk mixture, sour cream and yogurt, mixing until the batter is smooth and well-combined. Stir in the vanilla by hand. Fold in the mango and cherries.

5. Remove the springform pan from the freezer. Pour the batter into the pan and smooth with a rubber spatula.

6. Place the pan on the center rack of the oven and bake until the cheesecake sets and is lightly brown. If the cake begins to brown too quickly, cover the top loosely with aluminum foil. The cheesecake is done when the center of the cake is firm to the touch.

7. Remove the cake from the oven and place on a wire rack until completely cool (about 2 hours). Once cool, refrigerate for at least 2 hours. When chilled, the cheesecake will come out of the pan easily.

8. Before removing the pan, loosen the cake from the sides with a knife or metal spatula.

9. Spoon the whipped topping into a pastry bag and pipe rosettes along the edge of the cheesecake. Place a cherry on top of each rosette.

10. Cut into wedges and serve.

Creamy Eggnog Cheesecake

INGREDIENT	FOR 6-INCH CAKE	FOR 9-INCH CAKE
Fat-free cream cheese, softened	3 8-ounce packages	6 8-ounce packages
Sugar	¾ cup	1½ cups
Fat-free egg substitute	4 ounces	8 ounces
Nonfat powdered milk	¼ cup mixed with 2 tablespoons water	½ cup mixed with ¼ cup water
Fat-free sour cream	¼ cup	½ cup
Fat-free margarine, melted	¼ cup	½ cup
Dark rum	¼ cup	½ cup
All-purpose flour	¼ cup	½ cup
Vanilla extract	1 teaspoon	2 teaspoons
Nutmeg	1 teaspoon	2 teaspoons

CRUST

Graham Cracker (page 8)	single recipe	double recipe

GARNISH

Low-fat whipped topping	1 cup	2 cups
Freshly grated nutmeg	1 teaspoon	2 teaspoons

Baking Time	45–60 minutes	1¼–1½ hours
Serves	8	16
Calories per serving	269 (9 from fat)	269 (9 from fat)
Fat per serving	1 gram	1 gram

Rum-flavored eggnog is a holiday favorite. Now you can enjoy low-fat eggnog cheesecake during the holidays or on any occasion.

---

1. Preheat the oven to 350°F.

2. Gently pat the prepared crust mixture on the bottom and partially up the sides of a greased springform pan. Place in the freezer for 10 minutes.

3. Blend the cream cheese and sugar in an electric mixing bowl or food processor. Add the egg substitute and blend well.

4. Add the powdered milk mixture, sour cream, margarine, rum, and flour, mixing until the batter is smooth and well-combined. Stir in the vanilla and nutmeg by hand.

5. Remove the springform pan from the freezer. Pour the batter into the pan and smooth with a rubber spatula.

6. Place the pan on the center rack of the oven and bake until the cheesecake sets and is lightly brown. If the cake begins to brown too quickly, cover the top loosely with aluminum foil. The cheesecake is done when the center of the cake is firm to the touch.

7. Remove the cake from the oven and place on a wire rack until completely cool (about 2 hours). Once cool, refrigerate for at least 2 hours. When chilled, the cheesecake will come out of the pan easily.

8. Before removing the pan, loosen the cake from the sides with a knife or metal spatula.

9. Spoon the whipped topping into a pastry bag and pipe it decoratively on top of the cake. Dust with a sprinkling of nutmeg.

10. Cut into wedges and serve.

Perfect Pumpkin Cheesecake

INGREDIENT	FOR 6-INCH CAKE	FOR 9-INCH CAKE
Fat-free cream cheese, softened	3 8-ounce packages	6 8-ounce packages
Sugar	¾ cup	1½ cups
Fat-free egg substitute	4 ounces	8 ounces
Nonfat powdered milk	¼ cup mixed with 2 tablespoons water	½ cup mixed with ¼ cup water
Fat-free sour cream	¼ cup	½ cup
Fat-free margarine, melted	¼ cup	½ cup
Canned pumpkin	½ cup	1 cup
All-purpose flour	¼ cup	½ cup
Vanilla extract	1 teaspoon	2 teaspoons
Nutmeg	1 teaspoon	2 teaspoons
Ground cloves	¼ teaspoon	½ teaspoon

CRUST

Graham Cracker (page 8)	single recipe	double recipe

GARNISH

Low-fat whipped topping	1 cup	2 cups
Grated orange zest	1 teaspoon	2 teaspoons

Baking Time	45–60 minutes	1¼–1½ hours
Serves	8	16
Calories per serving	225 (9 from fat)	225 (9 from fat)
Fat per serving	1 gram	1 gram

This cheesecake is a delightful change from the traditional pumpkin pie.

---

1. Preheat the oven to 350°F.

2. Gently pat the prepared crust mixture on the bottom and partially up the sides of a greased springform pan. Place in the freezer for 10 minutes.

3. Blend the cream cheese and sugar in an electric mixing bowl or food processor. Add the egg substitute and blend well.

4. Add the powdered milk mixture, sour cream, margarine, pumpkin, and flour, mixing until the batter is smooth, light, and well combined. Stir in the vanilla, nutmeg, and cloves by hand.

5. Remove the springform pan from the freezer. Pour the batter into the pan and smooth with a rubber spatula.

6. Place the pan on the center rack of the oven and bake until the cheesecake sets and is lightly brown. If the cake begins to brown too quickly, cover the top loosely with aluminum foil. The cheesecake is done when the center of the cake is firm to the touch.

7. Remove the cake from the oven and place on a wire rack until completely cool (about 2 hours). Once cool, refrigerate for at least 2 hours. When chilled, the cheesecake will come out of the pan easily.

8. Before removing the pan, loosen the cake from the sides with a knife or metal spatula.

9. Spoon the whipped topping into a pastry bag and pipe it decoratively on top of the cake. Top with a sprinkling of orange zest.

10. Cut into wedges and serve.

Ginger Snap Cheesecake

INGREDIENT	FOR 6-INCH CAKE	FOR 9-INCH CAKE
Fat-free cream cheese, softened	3 8-ounce packages	6 8-ounce packages
Sugar	¾ cup	1½ cups
Fat-free egg substitute	4 ounces	8 ounces
Nonfat powdered milk	¼ cup mixed with 2 tablespoons water	½ cup mixed with ¼ cup water
Fat-free sour cream	¼ cup	½ cup
Fat-free margarine, melted	¼ cup	½ cup
All-purpose flour	¼ cup	½ cup
Ground ginger	2 teaspoons	4 teaspoons
Vanilla extract	1 teaspoon	2 teaspoons

CRUST

Graham Cracker (page 9)	single recipe	double recipe

GARNISH

Low-fat whipped topping	1 cup	2 cups
Candied ginger, coarsely chopped	¼ cup	½ cup

Baking Time	45–60 minutes	1¼–1½ hours
Serves	8	16
Calories per serving	227 (9 from fat)	227 (9 from fat)
Fat per serving	1 gram	1 gram

Center Left: Double Chocolate Mocha Cheesecake cupcakes (page 86)

Center Right: Classic Cherry Cheesecake (page 54)

Bottom: Butterscotch Sundae Cheesecake (page 142)

FLAVORS

Cherry
Butterscotch
Double Chocolate
Mocha
Vanilla
Chocolate
Strawberry
Floats, Sodas, Sund...
Enjoy

Top: **Creamy Kahlua Cheesecake** (page 112)

Left: **Piña Colada Cheesecake** (page 52)

Right: **No-Bake Lime Cheesecake** (page 244)

Flavorful ginger has the starring role in this delicious cheesecake.

---

1. Preheat the oven to 350°F.

2. Gently pat the prepared crust mixture on the bottom and partially up the sides of a greased springform pan. Place in the freezer for 10 minutes.

3. Blend the cream cheese and sugar in an electric mixing bowl or food processor. Add the egg substitute and blend well.

4. Add the powdered milk mixture, sour cream, margarine, and flour, mixing until the batter is smooth and well-combined. Stir in the ginger and vanilla by hand.

5. Remove the springform pan from the freezer. Pour the batter into the pan and smooth with a rubber spatula.

6. Place the pan on the center rack of the oven and bake until the cheesecake sets and is lightly brown. If the cake begins to brown too quickly, cover the top loosely with aluminum foil. The cheesecake is done when the center of the cake is firm to the touch.

7. Remove the cake from the oven and place on a wire rack until completely cool (about 2 hours). Once cool, refrigerate for at least 2 hours. When chilled, the cheesecake will come out of the pan easily.

8. Before removing the pan, loosen the cake from the sides with a knife or metal spatula.

9. Spoon the whipped topping into a pastry bag and pipe it decoratively on top of the cake. Top with candied ginger.

10. Cut into wedges and serve.

Rum Raisin Cheesecake

INGREDIENT	FOR 6-INCH CAKE	FOR 9-INCH CAKE
Fat-free cream cheese, softened	3 8-ounce packages	6 8-ounce packages
Honey	½ cup	1 cup
Fat-free egg substitute	4 ounces	8 ounces
Nonfat powdered milk	¼ cup mixed with 2 tablespoons water	½ cup mixed with ¼ cup water
Fat-free sour cream	¼ cup	½ cup
Fat-free margarine, melted	¼ cup	½ cup
Dark rum	¼ cup	½ cup
All-purpose flour	¼ cup	½ cup
Vanilla extract	1 teaspoon	2 teaspoons
Dark raisins	½ cup	1 cup

CRUST

Graham Cracker (page 8)	single recipe	double recipe

GARNISH

Low-fat whipped topping	1 cup	2 cups
Rum-soaked raisins	8	16

Baking Time	45–60 minutes	1¼–1½ hours
Serves	8	16
Calories per serving	288 (9 from fat)	288 (9 from fat)
Fat per serving	1 gram	1 gram

This rum-flavored treat is great to enjoy on a cold, blustery day.

---

1. Preheat the oven to 350°F.

2. Gently pat the prepared crust mixture on the bottom and partially up the sides of a greased springform pan. Place in the freezer for 10 minutes.

3. Blend the cream cheese and honey in an electric mixing bowl or food processor. Add the egg substitute and blend well.

4. Add the powdered milk mixture, sour cream, margarine, rum, and flour, mixing until the batter is smooth and well-combined. Stir in the vanilla by hand. Fold in the raisins.

5. Remove the springform pan from the freezer. Pour the batter into the pan and smooth with a rubber spatula.

6. Place the pan on the center rack of the oven and bake until the cheesecake sets and is lightly brown. If the cake begins to brown too quickly, cover the top loosely with aluminum foil. The cheesecake is done when the center of the cake is firm to the touch.

7. Remove the cake from the oven and place on a wire rack until completely cool (about 2 hours). Once cool, refrigerate for at least 2 hours. When chilled, the cheesecake will come out of the pan easily.

8. Before removing the pan, loosen the cake from the sides with a knife or metal spatula.

9. Spoon the whipped topping into a pastry bag and pipe rosettes along the top edge of the cake. Place a rum-soaked raisin on each.

10. Cut into wedges and serve.

Rose Petal Cheesecake

INGREDIENT	FOR 6-INCH CAKE	FOR 9-INCH CAKE
Fat-free cream cheese, softened	3 8-ounce packages	6 8-ounce packages
Honey	½ cup	1 cup
Fat-free egg substitute	4 ounces	8 ounces
Nonfat powdered milk	¼ cup mixed with 2 tablespoons water	½ cup mixed with ¼ cup water
Fat-free sour cream	¼ cup	½ cup
Fat-free margarine, melted	¼ cup	½ cup
Rose syrup*	½ cup	1 cup
Red food coloring	2 drops	4 drops
All-purpose flour	¼ cup	½ cup
Fresh lemon juice	1 tablespoon	2 tablespoons

CRUST

Graham Cracker (page 8)	single recipe	double recipe

GARNISH

Low-fat whipped topping	1 cup	2 cups
Pink roses with 2-inch stems and leaves attached	2 or 3	3 or 4

* Rose syrup is available in Greek and Middle Eastern markets. To make your own, see recipe on page 154.

Baking Time	45–60 minutes	1¼–1½ hours
Serves	8	16
Calories per serving	220 (9 from fat)	220 (9 from fat)
Fat per serving	1 gram	1 gram

Rose syrup gives this delicate-flavored cheesecake its unusual taste.

---

1. Preheat the oven to 350°F.

2. Gently pat the prepared crust mixture on the bottom and partially up the sides of a greased springform pan. Place in the freezer for 10 minutes.

3. Blend the cream cheese and honey in an electric mixing bowl or food processor. Add the egg substitute and blend well.

4. Add the powdered milk mixture, sour cream, margarine, rose syrup, food coloring, and flour. Mix until the batter is smooth and well-combined. Stir in the lemon juice by hand.

5. Remove the springform pan from the freezer. Pour the batter into the pan and smooth with a rubber spatula.

6. Place the pan on the center rack of the oven and bake until the cheesecake sets and is lightly brown. If the cake begins to brown too quickly, cover the top loosely with aluminum foil. The cheesecake is done when the center of the cake is firm to the touch.

7. Remove the cake from the oven and place on a wire rack until completely cool (about 2 hours). Once cool, refrigerate for at least 2 hours. When chilled, the cheesecake will come out of the pan easily.

8. Before removing the pan, loosen the cake from the sides with a knife or metal spatula.

9. Arrange the roses decoratively on the center of the cake and pipe whipped topping along the edge.

10. Cut into wedges and serve.

Butterscotch Sundae

INGREDIENT	FOR 6-INCH CAKE	FOR 9-INCH CAKE
Fat-free cream cheese, softened	3 8-ounce packages	6 8-ounce packages
Sugar	¾ cup	1½ cups
Fat-free egg substitute	4 ounces	8 ounces
Nonfat powdered milk	¼ cup mixed with 2 tablespoons water	½ cup mixed with ¼ cup water
Fat-free sour cream	¼ cup	½ cup
Fat-free margarine, melted	¼ cup	½ cup
Fat-free butterscotch ice cream topping	⅓ cup	⅔ cup
All-purpose flour	¼ cup	½ cup
Butterscotch flavoring	1 teaspoon	2 teaspoons
Vanilla extract	1 teaspoon	2 teaspoons

CRUST

Graham Cracker (page 8)	single recipe	double recipe

GARNISH

Low-fat whipped topping	1 cup	2 cups
Butterscotch flavoring	½ teaspoon	1 teaspoon
Butterscotch candy, crushed	¼ cup	½ cup

Baking Time	45–60 minutes	1¼–1½ hours
Serves	8	16
Calories per serving	281 (9 from fat)	281 (9 from fat)
Fat per serving	1 gram	1 gram

If you like butterscotch pudding, you'll love this flavorful cheesecake.

---

1. Preheat the oven to 350°F.

2. Gently pat the prepared crust mixture on the bottom and partially up the sides of a greased springform pan. Place in the freezer for 10 minutes.

3. Blend the cream cheese and sugar in an electric mixing bowl or food processor. Add the egg substitute and blend well.

4. Add the powdered milk mixture, sour cream, margarine, butterscotch topping, and flour, mixing until the batter is smooth and well-combined. Gently stir in the butterscotch flavoring and vanilla by hand.

5. Remove the springform pan from the freezer. Pour the batter into the pan and smooth with a rubber spatula.

6. Place the pan on the center rack of the oven and bake until the cheesecake sets and is lightly brown. If the cake begins to brown too quickly, cover the top loosely with aluminum foil. The cheesecake is done when the center of the cake is firm to the touch.

7. Remove the cake from the oven and place on a wire rack until completely cool (about 2 hours). Once cool, refrigerate for at least 2 hours. When chilled, the cheesecake will come out of the pan easily.

8. Before removing the pan, loosen the cake from the sides with a knife or metal spatula.

9. To garnish, fold the butterscotch flavoring into the whipped topping and spoon on top of the cake. Sprinkle with crushed butterscotch candy.

10. Cut into wedges and serve.

Peppermint Patty Cheesecake

INGREDIENT	FOR 6-INCH CAKE	FOR 9-INCH CAKE
Fat-free cream cheese, softened	3 8-ounce packages	6 8-ounce packages
Sugar	¾ cup	1½ cups
Fat-free egg substitute	4 ounces	8 ounces
Nonfat powdered milk	¼ cup mixed with 2 tablespoons water	½ cup mixed with ¼ cup water
Fat-free sour cream	¼ cup	½ cup
Fat-free margarine, melted	¼ cup	½ cup
All-purpose flour	¼ cup	½ cup
Peppermint extract	1 teaspoon	2 teaspoons
Vanilla extract	1 teaspoon	2 teaspoons
Red food coloring	2 drops	4 drops

CRUST

Graham Cracker (page 8)	single recipe	double recipe

GARNISH

Low-fat whipped topping	1 cup	2 cups
Peppermint candies, crushed	2 tablespoons	¼ cup

Baking Time	45–60 minutes	1¼–1½ hours
Serves	8	16
Calories per serving	220 (9 from fat)	220 (9 from fat)
Fat per serving	1 gram	1 gram

Enjoy the tingling taste of peppermint in this cool, creamy dessert.

1. Preheat the oven to 350°F.

2. Gently pat the prepared crust mixture on the bottom and partially up the sides of a greased springform pan. Place in the freezer for 10 minutes.

3. Blend the cream cheese and sugar in an electric mixing bowl or food processor. Add the egg substitute and blend well.

4. Add the powdered milk mixture, sour cream, margarine, and flour, mixing until the batter is smooth and well-combined. Gently stir in the peppermint and vanilla extracts and food coloring by hand.

5. Remove the springform pan from the freezer. Pour the batter into the pan and smooth with a rubber spatula.

6. Place the pan on the center rack of the oven and bake until the cheesecake sets and is lightly brown. If the cake begins to brown too quickly, cover the top loosely with aluminum foil. The cheesecake is done when the center of the cake is firm to the touch.

7. Remove the cake from the oven and place on a wire rack until completely cool (about 2 hours). Once cool, refrigerate for at least 2 hours. When chilled, the cheesecake will come out of the pan easily.

8. Before removing the pan, loosen the cake from the sides with a knife or metal spatula.

9. Spoon the whipped topping on the cake and top with the crushed candy.

10. Cut into wedges and serve.

Creamy Caramel Cheesecake

INGREDIENT	FOR 6-INCH CAKE	FOR 9-INCH CAKE
Fat-free cream cheese, softened	3 8-ounce packages	6 8-ounce packages
Sugar	¾ cup	1½ cups
Fat-free egg substitute	4 ounces	8 ounces
Nonfat powdered milk	¼ cup mixed with 2 tablespoons water	½ cup mixed with ¼ cup water
Fat-free sour cream	¼ cup	½ cup
Fat-free margarine, melted	¼ cup	½ cup
Fat-free caramel ice cream topping	⅓ cup	⅔ cup
All-purpose flour	¼ cup	½ cup
Vanilla extract	1 teaspoon	2 teaspoons
CRUST		
Chocolate Graham Cracker (page 10)	single recipe	double recipe
GARNISH		
Low-fat whipped topping	1 cup	2 cups
European-style cocoa	1 teaspoon	2 teaspoons

Baking Time	45–60 minutes	1¼–1½ hours
Serves	8	16
Calories per serving	254 (9 from fat)	254 (9 from fat)
Fat per serving	1 gram	1 gram

The rich, creamy taste of caramel is highlighted in this luscious cheesecake.

---

1. Preheat the oven to 350°F.

2. Gently pat the prepared crust mixture on the bottom and partially up the sides of a greased springform pan. Place in the freezer for 10 minutes.

3. Blend the cream cheese and sugar in an electric mixing bowl or food processor. Add the egg substitute and blend well.

4. Add the powdered milk mixture, sour cream, margarine, caramel topping, and flour, mixing until the batter is smooth and well-combined. Gently stir in the butterscotch flavoring and vanilla by hand.

5. Remove the springform pan from the freezer. Pour the batter into the pan and smooth with a rubber spatula.

6. Place the pan on the center rack of the oven and bake until the cheesecake sets and is lightly brown. If the cake begins to brown too quickly, cover the top loosely with aluminum foil. The cheesecake is done when the center of the cake is firm to the touch.

7. Remove the cake from the oven and place on a wire rack until completely cool (about 2 hours). Once cool, refrigerate for at least 2 hours. When chilled, the cheesecake will come out of the pan easily.

8. Before removing the pan, loosen the cake from the sides with a knife or metal spatula.

9. To garnish, fold the butterscotch flavoring into the whipped topping and spoon on top of the cake. Sprinkle with crushed butterscotch candy.

10. Cut into wedges and serve.

Baklava Cheesecake

INGREDIENT	FOR 6-INCH CAKE	FOR 9-INCH CAKE
Fat-free cream cheese, softened	3 8-ounce packages	6 8-ounce packages
Honey	½ cup	1 cup
Fat-free egg substitute	4 ounces	8 ounces
Nonfat powdered milk	¼ cup mixed with 2 tablespoons water	½ cup mixed with ¼ cup water
Fat-free sour cream	¼ cup	½ cup
Fat-free margarine, melted	¼ cup	½ cup
All-purpose flour	¼ cup	½ cup
Fresh lemon juice	1 tablespoon	2 tablespoons
Walnut extract	1 teaspoon	2 teaspoons
Vanilla extract	1 teaspoon	2 teaspoons
Rose water	1 teaspoon	2 teaspoons
CRUST		
Flaky Phyllo (page 34)	single recipe	double recipe
GARNISH		
Low-fat whipped topping	1 cup	2 cups
Chopped walnuts	1 teaspoon	2 teaspoons

Baking Time	45–60 minutes	1¼–1½ hours
Serves	8	16
Calories per serving	226 (9 from fat)	226 (9 from fat)
Fat per serving	1 gram	1 gram

This exotic cheesecake was inspired by a traditional Greek pastry.

---

1. Preheat the oven to 350°F.

2. Prepare the phyllo crust in the appropriate sized greased springform pan and set aside.

3. Blend the cream cheese and honey in an electric mixing bowl or food processor. Add the egg substitute and blend well.

4. Add the powdered milk mixture, sour cream, margarine, and flour, mixing until the batter is smooth and well-combined. Gently stir in the lemon juice, walnut and vanilla extracts, and rose water by hand.

5. Pour the batter into the pan and smooth with a rubber spatula.

6. Place the pan on the center rack of the oven and bake until the cheesecake sets and is lightly brown. If the cake begins to brown too quickly, cover the top loosely with aluminum foil. The cheesecake is done when the center of the cake is firm to the touch.

7. Remove the cake from the oven and place on a wire rack until completely cool (about 2 hours). Once cool, refrigerate for at least 2 hours. When chilled, the cheesecake will come out of the pan easily.

8. Before removing the pan, loosen the cake from the sides with a knife or metal spatula.

9. Garnish with whipped topping and chopped walnuts.

10. Cut into wedges and serve.

Cookies-and-Cream Cheesecake

INGREDIENT	FOR 6-INCH CAKE	FOR 9-INCH CAKE
Fat-free cream cheese, softened	3 8-ounce packages	6 8-ounce packages
Sugar	¾ cup	1½ cups
Fat-free egg substitute	4 ounces	8 ounces
Nonfat powdered milk	¼ cup mixed with 2 tablespoons water	½ cup mixed with ¼ cup water
Fat-free sour cream	¼ cup	½ cup
Fat-free margarine, melted	¼ cup	½ cup
All-purpose flour	¼ cup	½ cup
Fresh lemon juice	1 tablespoon	2 tablespoons
Vanilla extract	1 teaspoon	2 teaspoons
Low-fat chocolate sandwich cookies, crushed	6	12

CRUST

Chocolate Graham Cracker (page 10)	single recipe	double recipe

GARNISH

Low-fat whipped topping	1 cup	2 cups
Low-fat chocolate sandwich cookies, separated	4	8

Baking Time	45–60 minutes	1¼–1½ hours
Serves	8	16
Calories per serving	271 (17 from fat)	271 (17 from fat)
Fat per serving	1.9 grams	1.9 grams

Here's a cheesecake in honor of my favorite ice cream flavor.

---

1. Preheat the oven to 350°F.

2. Gently pat the prepared crust mixture on the bottom and partially up the sides of a greased springform pan. Place in the freezer for 10 minutes.

3. Blend the cream cheese and sugar in an electric mixing bowl or food processor. Add the egg substitute and blend well.

4. Add the powdered milk mixture, sour cream, margarine, and flour, mixing until the batter is smooth and well-combined. Stir in the lemon juice and vanilla by hand. Fold in the crushed cookies.

5. Remove the springform pan from the freezer. Pour the batter into the pan and smooth with a rubber spatula.

6. Place the pan on the center rack of the oven and bake until the cheesecake sets and is lightly brown. If the cake begins to brown too quickly, cover the top loosely with aluminum foil. The cheesecake is done when the center of the cake is firm to the touch.

7. Remove the cake from the oven and place on a wire rack until completely cool (about 2 hours). Once cool, refrigerate for at least 2 hours. When chilled, the cheesecake will come out of the pan easily.

8. Before removing the pan, loosen the cake from the sides with a knife or metal spatula.

9. Spoon the whipped topping into a pastry bag and pipe rosettes along the top of the cake. Separate the sandwich cookies in half, and place the halves between the rosettes.

10. Cut into wedges and serve.

Variations

You can easily make this cheesecake using chocolate chip or peanut butter cookies.

Coffee Bean Cheesecake

INGREDIENT	FOR 6-INCH CAKE	FOR 9-INCH CAKE
Fat-free cream cheese, softened	2 8-ounce packages	4 8-ounce packages
Firm tofu, mashed	8 ounces	16 ounces
Honey	$\frac{1}{4}$ cup	1 cup
Fat-free egg substitute	4 ounces	8 ounces
Nonfat powdered milk	$\frac{1}{4}$ cup mixed with 2 tablespoons water	$\frac{1}{2}$ cup mixed with $\frac{1}{4}$ cup water
Fat-free sour cream	$\frac{1}{4}$ cup	$\frac{1}{2}$ cup
Fat-free yogurt	$\frac{1}{4}$ cup	$\frac{1}{2}$ cup
Strong-brewed coffee or espresso	$\frac{1}{4}$ cup	$\frac{1}{2}$ cup
Vanilla extract	1 teaspoon	2 teaspoons
Mini coffee jelly beans	$\frac{1}{2}$ cup	1 cup

CRUST

Graham Cracker (page 8)	single recipe	double recipe

GARNISH

Low-fat whipped topping	1 cup	2 cups
Instant coffee granules	2 tablespoons	$\frac{1}{4}$ cup
Espresso powder	1 teaspoon	2 teaspoons

Baking Time	45–60 minutes	$1\frac{1}{4}$–$1\frac{1}{2}$ hours
Serves	8	16
Calories per serving	249 (25 from fat)	249 (25 from fat)
Fat per serving	2.75 grams	2.75 grams

Jelly beans lend an unusual—and pleasant—addition to this cheesecake.

___

1. Preheat the oven to 350°F.

2. Gently pat the prepared crust mixture on the bottom and partially up the sides of a greased springform pan. Place in the freezer for 10 minutes.

3. Blend the cream cheese, tofu, and sugar in an electric mixer or food processor. Add the egg substitute and blend well.

4. Add the powdered milk mixture, sour cream, yogurt, and espresso, mixing until the batter is smooth and well-combined. Stir in the vanilla by hand. Fold in the jelly beans.

5. Remove the springform pan from the freezer. Pour the batter into the pan and smooth with a rubber spatula.

6. Place the pan on the center rack of the oven and bake until the cheesecake sets and is lightly brown. If the cake begins to brown too quickly, cover the top loosely with aluminum foil. The cheesecake is done when the center of the cake is firm to the touch.

7. Remove the cake from the oven and place on a wire rack until completely cool (about 2 hours). Once cool, refrigerate for at least 2 hours. When chilled, the cheesecake will come out of the pan easily.

8. Before removing the pan, loosen the cake from the sides with a knife or metal spatula.

9. To garnish, fold the coffee granules into the whipped topping and spoon on top of the cake. Dust with espresso powder.

10. Cut into wedges and serve.

Making Rose Syrup

Delicate-flavored rose syrup is used to flavor a number of the cheesecakes offered in this book, including Rose Petal (page 140), and Roses and Cream (page 200). If you have access to a rose garden, you may wish to try the following recipe, which yields about 1½ cups.

1 cup water
½ cup honey
2 teaspoons rose water
1 cup (about 20) rose petals, clean, dry, and highly scented
1 drop red food coloring (optional)

1. Place the water, honey, and rose water in a saucepan over medium heat and stir constantly until the honey is dissolved. Reduce the heat and simmer 5 minutes.

2. Add the rose petals and simmer another 3 minutes. Remove from the heat, add the food coloring, and allow the mixture to sit 2 hours.

3. Pour the cooled syrup through a strainer, pressing the rose petals to extract all of their flavor.

4. Transfer to a tightly sealed container and store in the refrigerator where it will keep for two weeks.

8.

Light and Lovely Layers

Can't decide which cheesecake flavor to try? Why not try two, or even three flavors at once? Simply divide a basic batter in half or thirds, then add your favorite flavoring to each portion. Carefully layer the batters and bake as usual.

The layered flavors in this chapter are among my favorites. You'll find sweet juicy cherries and creamy rich chocolate in the Chocolate Cherry Cheesecake (page 170), as well as an equally luscious Orange Creamsicle Cheesecake (page186), which brings together the sweet tang of oranges and the velvety smoothness of classic vanilla. There are other blue-ribbon combinations such as Pineapple with Coconut Cream (page 192), Café au Lait (page 182), and Root Beer Float (page 180). And the list goes on and on.

Whether you try the recipes as written or create your own layer combinations, be prepared for cheesecakes that are easy, elegant, and delicious.

Triple Treat Cheesecake

INGREDIENT	FOR 6-INCH CAKE	FOR 9-INCH CAKE
Fat-free cream cheese, softened	3 8-ounce packages	6 8-ounce packages
Sugar	¾ cup	1½ cups
Fat-free egg substitute	4 ounces	8 ounces
Nonfat powdered milk	¼ cup mixed with 2 tablespoons water	½ cup mixed with ¼ cup water
Fat-free sour cream	¼ cup	½ cup
Fat-free margarine, melted	¼ cup	½ cup
All-purpose flour	¼ cup	½ cup
Fresh lemon juice	1 tablespoon	2 tablespoons
Vanilla extract	1 teaspoon	2 teaspoons
European-style cocoa	½ cup	1 cup
Puréed strawberries, fresh or frozen*	½ cup	1 cup

CRUST

Chocolate Graham Cracker (page 10)	single recipe	double recipe

GARNISH

Low-fat whipped topping	1 cup	2 cups
Strawberries, sliced	½ cup	1 cup

* Be sure to thaw and drain if using frozen variety.

Baking time	45–60 minutes	1¼–1½ hours
Serves	8	16
Calories per serving	228 (13 from fat)	228 (13 from fat)
Fat per serving	1.5 grams	1.5 grams

Creamy vanilla, rich chocolate, and luscious strawberries—together in one cheesecake!

---

1. Preheat the oven to 350°F.

2. Gently pat the prepared crust mixture on the bottom and partially up the sides of a greased springform pan. Place in the freezer for 10 minutes.

3. Blend the cream cheese and sugar in an electric mixing bowl or food processor. Add the egg substitute and blend well.

4. Add the powdered milk mixture, sour cream, margarine, and flour, mixing until the batter is smooth and well-combined. Stir in the lemon juice and vanilla by hand.

5. Divide the batter into thirds. Fold the cocoa into one third, the strawberries into another, and leave the last one plain.

6. Remove the springform pan from the freezer. Pour the cocoa batter into the pan and smooth with a rubber spatula. Gently spoon the strawberry batter on top, then follow with the vanilla batter.

7. Place the pan on the center rack of the oven and bake until the cheesecake sets and is lightly brown. If the cake begins to brown too quickly, cover the top loosely with aluminum foil. The cheesecake is done when the center of the cake is firm to the touch.

8. Remove the cake from the oven and place on a wire rack until completely cool (about 2 hours). Once cool, refrigerate for at least 2 hours. When chilled, the cheesecake will come out of the pan easily.

9. Before removing the pan, loosen the cake from the sides with a knife or metal spatula.

10. Spoon the topping into a pastry bag and pipe it decoratively on top of the cake. Top with sliced strawberries.

11. Cut into wedges and serve.

Chocolate and Cream Cheesecake

INGREDIENT	FOR 6-INCH CAKE	FOR 9-INCH CAKE
Fat-free cream cheese, softened	3 8-ounce packages	6 8-ounce packages
Sugar	¾ cup	1½ cups
Fat-free egg substitute	4 ounces	8 ounces
Nonfat powdered milk	¼ cup mixed with 2 tablespoons water	½ cup mixed with ¼ cup water
Fat-free sour cream	¼ cup	½ cup
Fat-free margarine, melted	¼ cup	½ cup
All-purpose flour	¼ cup	½ cup
Fresh lemon juice	1 tablespoon	2 tablespoons
Vanilla extract	1 teaspoon	2 teaspoons
European-style cocoa	½ cup	1 cup

CRUST

Graham Cracker (page 8)	single recipe	double recipe

GARNISH

Low-fat whipped topping	1 cup	2 cups
European-style cocoa	1 teaspoon	2 teaspoons

Baking time	45–60 minutes	1¼–1½ hours
Serves	8	16
Calories per serving	228 (13 from fat)	228 (13 from fat)
Fat per serving	1.5 grams	1.5 grams

If you are a fan of chocolate cream pie like I am, this low-fat chocolate and cream cheesecake is for you.

---

1. Preheat the oven to 350°F.

2. Gently pat the prepared crust mixture on the bottom and partially up the sides of a greased springform pan. Place in the freezer for 10 minutes.

3. Blend the cream cheese and sugar in an electric mixing bowl or food processor. Add the egg substitute and blend well.

4. Add the powdered milk mixture, sour cream, margarine, and flour, mixing until the batter is smooth and well-combined. Stir in the lemon juice and vanilla by hand.

5. Divide the batter in half. Fold the cocoa into one half, and leave the other half plain.

6. Remove the springform pan from the freezer. Pour the cocoa batter into the pan and smooth with a rubber spatula. Gently spoon the vanilla batter on top.

7. Place the pan on the center rack of the oven and bake until the cheesecake sets and is lightly brown. If the cake begins to brown too quickly, cover the top loosely with aluminum foil. The cheesecake is done when the center of the cake is firm to the touch.

8. Remove the cake from the oven and place on a wire rack until completely cool (about 2 hours). Once cool, refrigerate for at least 2 hours. When chilled, the cheesecake will come out of the pan easily.

9. Before removing the pan, loosen the cake from the sides with a knife or metal spatula.

10. Spoon the topping into a pastry bag and pipe it decoratively on top of the cake. Dust with cocoa.

11. Cut into wedges and serve.

Chocolate Hazelnut Cheesecake

INGREDIENT	FOR 6-INCH CAKE	FOR 9-INCH CAKE
Fat-free cream cheese, softened	3 8-ounce packages	6 8-ounce packages
Sugar	¾ cup	1½ cups
Fat-free egg substitute	4 ounces	8 ounces
Nonfat powdered milk	¼ cup mixed with 2 tablespoons water	½ cup mixed with ¼ cup water
Fat-free sour cream	¼ cup	½ cup
Fat-free margarine, melted	¼ cup	½ cup
All-purpose flour	¼ cup	½ cup
Fresh lemon juice	1 tablespoon	2 tablespoons
Vanilla extract	1 teaspoon	2 teaspoons
European-style cocoa	⅓ cup	⅔ cup
Hazelnut extract	1 teaspoon	2 teaspoons

CRUST

Graham Cracker (page 8)	single recipe	double recipe

GARNISH

Low-fat whipped topping	1 cup	2 cups
European-style cocoa	1 teaspoon	2 teaspoons

Baking time	45–60 minutes	1¼–1½ hours
Serves	8	16
Calories per serving	253 (36 from fat)	253 (36 from fat)
Fat per serving	4 grams	4 grams

A perfect choice for special occasions.

---

1. Preheat the oven to 350°F.

2. Gently pat the prepared crust mixture on the bottom and partially up the sides of a greased springform pan. Place in the freezer for 10 minutes.

3. Blend the cream cheese and sugar in an electric mixing bowl or food processor. Add the egg substitute and blend well.

4. Add the powdered milk mixture, sour cream, margarine, and flour, mixing until the batter is smooth and well-combined. Stir in the lemon juice and vanilla by hand.

5. Divide the batter in half. Fold the cocoa into one half, and the hazelnut extract into the other.

6. Remove the springform pan from the freezer. Pour the cocoa batter into the pan and smooth with a rubber spatula. Gently spoon the hazelnut batter on top.

7. Place the pan on the center rack of the oven and bake until the cheesecake sets and is lightly brown. If the cake begins to brown too quickly, cover the top loosely with aluminum foil. The cheesecake is done when the center of the cake is firm to the touch.

8. Remove the cake from the oven and place on a wire rack until completely cool (about 2 hours). Once cool, refrigerate for at least 2 hours. When chilled, the cheesecake will come out of the pan easily.

9. Before removing the pan, loosen the cake from the sides with a knife or metal spatula.

10. Spoon the topping decoratively on top of the cake and dust with cocoa.

11. Cut into wedges and serve.

Chocolate Mint Cheesecake

INGREDIENT	FOR 6-INCH CAKE	FOR 9-INCH CAKE
Fat-free cream cheese, softened	3 8-ounce packages	6 8-ounce packages
Sugar	¾ cup	1½ cups
Fat-free egg substitute	4 ounces	8 ounces
Nonfat powdered milk	¼ cup mixed with 2 tablespoons water	½ cup mixed with ¼ cup water
Fat-free sour cream	¼ cup	½ cup
Fat-free margarine, melted	¼ cup	½ cup
All-purpose flour	¼ cup	½ cup
Fresh lemon juice	1 tablespoon	2 tablespoons
Vanilla extract	1 teaspoon	2 teaspoons
European-style cocoa	⅓ cup	⅔ cup
Mint extract	2 teaspoon	4 teaspoons
Green food coloring	2 drops	4 drops

CRUST

Chocolate Graham Cracker (page 10)	single recipe	double recipe

GARNISH

Low-fat whipped topping	1 cup	2 cups
European-style cocoa	1 teaspoon	2 teaspoons
Mint leaves	5–7	7–9

Baking time	45–60 minutes	1¼–1½ hours
Serves	8	16
Calories per serving	229 (14 from fat)	229 (14 from fat)
Fat per serving	1.6 grams	1.6 grams

This minty cool cheesecake is as beautiful as it is delicious.

---

1. Preheat the oven to 350°F.

2. Gently pat the prepared crust mixture on the bottom and partially up the sides of a greased springform pan. Place in the freezer for 10 minutes.

3. Blend the cream cheese and sugar in an electric mixing bowl or food processor. Add the egg substitute and blend well.

4. Add the powdered milk mixture, sour cream, margarine, and flour, mixing until the batter is smooth and well-combined. Stir in the lemon juice and vanilla by hand.

5. Divide the batter in half. Fold the cocoa into one half, and the mint and food coloring into the other.

6. Remove the springform pan from the freezer. Pour the cocoa batter into the pan and smooth with a rubber spatula. Gently spoon the mint batter on top.

7. Place the pan on the center rack of the oven and bake until the cheesecake sets and is lightly brown. If the cake begins to brown too quickly, cover the top loosely with aluminum foil. The cheesecake is done when the center of the cake is firm to the touch.

8. Remove the cake from the oven and place on a wire rack until completely cool (about 2 hours). Once cool, refrigerate for at least 2 hours. When chilled, the cheesecake will come out of the pan easily.

9. Before removing the pan, loosen the cake from the sides with a knife or metal spatula.

10. Spoon the topping on the cake, dust with cocoa, and decorate with mint leaves.

11. Cut into wedges and serve.

Peanut Butter Cup Cheesecake

INGREDIENT	FOR 6-INCH CAKE	FOR 9-INCH CAKE
Fat-free cream cheese, softened	3 8-ounce packages	6 8-ounce packages
Sugar	¾ cup	1½ cups
Fat-free egg substitute	4 ounces	8 ounces
Nonfat powdered milk	¼ cup mixed with 2 tablespoons water	½ cup mixed with ¼ cup water
Fat-free sour cream	¼ cup	½ cup
Fat-free margarine, melted	¼ cup	½ cup
All-purpose flour	¼ cup	½ cup
Fresh lemon juice	1 tablespoon	2 tablespoons
Vanilla extract	1 teaspoon	2 teaspoons
European-style cocoa	⅓ cup	⅔ cup
Reduced-fat peanut butter	¼ cup	½ cup

CRUST

Graham Cracker (page 8)	single recipe	double recipe

GARNISH

Low-fat whipped topping	1 cup	2 cups
European-style cocoa	1 teaspoon	2 teaspoons

Baking time	45–60 minutes	1¼–1½ hours
Serves	8	16
Calories per serving	274 (41 from fat)	274 (41 from fat)
Fat per serving	4.6 grams	4.6 grams

An all-time favorite combination of chocolate and peanut butter in a rich creamy cheesecake.

---

1. Preheat the oven to 350°F.

2. Gently pat the prepared crust mixture on the bottom and partially up the sides of a greased springform pan. Place in the freezer for 10 minutes.

3. Blend the cream cheese and sugar in an electric mixing bowl or food processor. Add the egg substitute and blend well.

4. Add the powdered milk mixture, sour cream, margarine, and flour, mixing until the batter is smooth and well-combined. Stir in the lemon juice and vanilla by hand.

5. Divide the batter in half. Fold the cocoa into one half, and the peanut butter into the other.

6. Remove the springform pan from the freezer. Pour the cocoa batter into the pan and smooth with a rubber spatula. Gently spoon the peanut butter layer on top.

7. Place the pan on the center rack of the oven and bake until the cheesecake sets and is lightly brown. If the cake begins to brown too quickly, cover the top loosely with aluminum foil. The cheesecake is done when the center of the cake is firm to the touch.

8. Remove the cake from the oven and place on a wire rack until completely cool (about 2 hours). Once cool, refrigerate for at least 2 hours. When chilled, the cheesecake will come out of the pan easily.

9. Before removing the pan, loosen the cake from the sides with a knife or metal spatula.

10. Spoon the whipped topping on the cake and dust with cocoa.

11. Cut into wedges and serve.

Chocolate Strawberry Cheesecake

INGREDIENT	FOR 6-INCH CAKE	FOR 9-INCH CAKE
Fat-free cream cheese, softened	3 8-ounce packages	6 8-ounce packages
Sugar	¾ cup	1½ cups
Fat-free egg substitute	4 ounces	8 ounces
Nonfat powdered milk	¼ cup mixed with 2 tablespoons water	½ cup mixed with ¼ cup water
Fat-free sour cream	¼ cup	½ cup
Fat-free margarine, melted	¼ cup	½ cup
All-purpose flour	¼ cup	½ cup
Fresh lemon juice	1 tablespoon	2 tablespoons
Vanilla extract	1 teaspoon	2 teaspoons
European-style cocoa	⅓ cup	⅔ cup
Puréed strawberries, fresh or frozen*	½ cup	1 cup

CRUST

Graham Cracker (page 8)	single recipe	double recipe

GARNISH

Low-fat whipped topping	1 cup	2 cups
European-style cocoa	1 teaspoon	2 teaspoons
Strawberries, sliced	½ cup	1 cup

* Be sure to thaw and drain if using frozen variety.

Baking time	45–60 minutes	1¼–1½ hours
Serves	8	16
Calories per serving	239 (13 from fat)	239 (13 from fat)
Fat per serving	1.5 grams	1.5 grams

Creamy chocolate and luscious strawberries combine to make this sensational layered cheesecake.

---

1. Preheat the oven to 350°F.

2. Gently pat the prepared crust mixture on the bottom and partially up the sides of a greased springform pan. Place in the freezer for 10 minutes.

3. Blend the cream cheese and sugar in an electric mixing bowl or food processor. Add the egg substitute and blend well.

4. Add the powdered milk mixture, sour cream, margarine, and flour, mixing until the batter is smooth and well-combined. Gently stir in the lemon juice and vanilla by hand.

5. Divide the batter in half. Fold the cocoa into one half, and the strawberries into the other.

6. Remove the springform pan from the freezer. Pour the cocoa batter into the pan and smooth with a rubber spatula. Gently spoon the strawberry layer on top.

7. Place the pan on the center rack of the oven and bake until the cheesecake sets and is lightly brown. If the cake begins to brown too quickly, cover the top loosely with aluminum foil. The cheesecake is done when the center of the cake is firm to the touch.

8. Remove the cake from the oven and place on a wire rack until completely cool (about 2 hours). Once cool, refrigerate for at least 2 hours. When chilled, the cheesecake will come out of the pan easily.

9. Before removing the pan, loosen the cake from the sides with a knife or metal spatula.

10. Spoon the whipped topping on the cake and dust with cocoa.

11. Cut into wedges and serve.

Orange and Chocolate Cheesecake

INGREDIENT	FOR 6-INCH CAKE	FOR 9-INCH CAKE
Fat-free cream cheese, softened	3 8-ounce packages	6 8-ounce packages
Sugar	¾ cup	1½ cups
Fat-free egg substitute	4 ounces	8 ounces
Nonfat powdered milk	¼ cup mixed with 2 tablespoons water	½ cup mixed with ¼ cup water
Fat-free sour cream	¼ cup	½ cup
Fat-free margarine, melted	¼ cup	½ cup
All-purpose flour	¼ cup	½ cup
Fresh lemon juice	1 tablespoon	2 tablespoons
Vanilla extract	1 teaspoon	2 teaspoons
European-style cocoa	¼ cup	½ cup
Orange extract	1 teaspoon	2 teaspoons

CRUST

Zesty Orange Graham Cracker (page 12)	single recipe	double recipe

GARNISH

Low-fat whipped topping	1 cup	2 cups
European-style cocoa	1 teaspoon	2 teaspoons
Grated orange zest	1 teaspoon	2 teaspoons

Baking time	45–60 minutes	1¼–1½ hours
Serves	8	16
Calories per serving	233 (13 from fat)	233 (13 from fat)
Fat per serving	1.5 grams	1.5 grams

Another classic flavor combination.

---

1. Preheat the oven to 350°F.

2. Gently pat the prepared crust mixture on the bottom and partially up the sides of a greased springform pan. Place in the freezer for 10 minutes.

3. Blend the cream cheese and sugar in an electric mixing bowl or food processor. Add the egg substitute and blend well.

4. Add the powdered milk mixture, sour cream, margarine, and flour, mixing until the batter is smooth and well-combined. Gently stir in the lemon juice and vanilla by hand.

5. Divide the batter in half. Fold the cocoa into one half, and the orange extract into the other.

6. Remove the springform pan from the freezer. Pour the cocoa batter into the pan and smooth with a rubber spatula. Gently spoon the orange layer on top.

7. Place the pan on the center rack of the oven and bake until the cheesecake sets and is lightly brown. If the cake begins to brown too quickly, cover the top loosely with aluminum foil. The cheesecake is done when the center of the cake is firm to the touch.

8. Remove the cake from the oven and place on a wire rack until completely cool (about 2 hours). Once cool, refrigerate for at least 2 hours. When chilled, the cheesecake will come out of the pan easily.

9. Before removing the pan, loosen the cake from the sides with a knife or metal spatula.

10. Spoon the whipped topping on the cake. Top with a dusting of cocoa and a sprinkling of orange zest.

11. Cut into wedges and serve.

Chocolate Cherry Cheesecake

INGREDIENT	FOR 6-INCH CAKE	FOR 9-INCH CAKE
Fat-free cream cheese, softened	3 8-ounce packages	6 8-ounce packages
Sugar	¾ cup	1½ cups
Fat-free egg substitute	4 ounces	8 ounces
Nonfat powdered milk	¼ cup mixed with 2 tablespoons water	½ cup mixed with ¼ cup water
Fat-free sour cream	¼ cup	½ cup
Fat-free margarine, melted	¼ cup	½ cup
All-purpose flour	¼ cup	½ cup
Fresh lemon juice	1 tablespoon	2 tablespoons
Vanilla extract	1 teaspoon	2 teaspoons
European-style cocoa	⅓ cup	⅔ cup
Puréed dark sweet cherries	½ cup	1 cup

CRUST

Graham Cracker (page 8)	single recipe	double recipe

GARNISH

Low-fat whipped topping	1 cup	2 cups
European-style cocoa	1 teaspoon	2 teaspoons
Dark sweet cherries, halved	½ cup	1 cup

Baking time	45–60 minutes	1¼–1½ hours
Serves	8	16
Calories per serving	248 (14 from fat)	248 (14 from fat)
Fat per serving	1.6 grams	1.6 grams

Rich cocoa and sweet cherries combine to make this cheesecake decadent and delicious.

___

1. Preheat the oven to 350°F.

2. Gently pat the prepared crust mixture on the bottom and partially up the sides of a greased springform pan. Place in the freezer for 10 minutes.

3. Blend the cream cheese and sugar in an electric mixing bowl or food processor. Add the egg substitute and blend well.

4. Add the powdered milk mixture, sour cream, margarine, and flour, mixing until the batter is smooth and well-combined. Gently stir in the lemon juice and vanilla by hand.

5. Divide the batter in half. Fold the cocoa into one half, and the puréed cherries into the other.

6. Remove the springform pan from the freezer. Pour the cocoa batter into the pan and smooth with a rubber spatula. Gently spoon the cherry layer on top.

7. Place the pan on the center rack of the oven and bake until the cheesecake sets and is lightly brown. If the cake begins to brown too quickly, cover the top loosely with aluminum foil. The cheesecake is done when the center of the cake is firm to the touch.

8. Remove the cake from the oven and place on a wire rack until completely cool (about 2 hours). Once cool, refrigerate for at least 2 hours. When chilled, the cheesecake will come out of the pan easily.

9. Before removing the pan, loosen the cake from the sides with a knife or metal spatula.

10. Spoon the whipped topping on the cake. Top with the cherry halves and a dusting of cocoa.

11. Cut into wedges and serve.

Strawberries and Cream Cheesecake

INGREDIENT	FOR 6-INCH CAKE	FOR 9-INCH CAKE
Fat-free cream cheese, softened	3 8-ounce packages	6 8-ounce packages
Honey	½ cup	1 cup
Fat-free egg substitute	4 ounces	8 ounces
Nonfat powdered milk	¼ cup mixed with 2 tablespoons water	½ cup mixed with ¼ cup water
Fat-free sour cream	¼ cup	½ cup
Fat-free margarine, melted	¼ cup	½ cup
All-purpose flour	¼ cup	½ cup
Fresh lemon juice	1 tablespoon	2 tablespoons
Vanilla extract	1 teaspoon	2 teaspoons
Puréed strawberries, fresh or frozen*	½ cup	1 cup

CRUST

Graham Cracker (page 8)	single recipe	double recipe

GARNISH

Low-fat whipped topping	1 cup	2 cups
Fresh strawberries, sliced	½ cup	1 cup

* Be sure to thaw and drain if using frozen variety.

Baking time	45–60 minutes	1¼–1½ hours
Serves	8	16
Calories per serving	228 (9 from fat)	228 (9 from fat)
Fat per serving	1 gram	1 gram

Classic flavors unite in this exquisite dessert.

---

1. Preheat the oven to 350°F.

2. Gently pat the prepared crust mixture on the bottom and partially up the sides of a greased springform pan. Place in the freezer for 10 minutes.

3. Blend the cream cheese and honey in an electric mixing bowl or food processor. Add the egg substitute and blend well.

4. Add the powdered milk mixture, sour cream, margarine, and flour, mixing until the batter is smooth and well-combined. Gently stir in the lemon juice and vanilla by hand.

5. Divide the batter in half. Fold the puréed strawberries into one half and leave the other half plain.

6. Remove the springform pan from the freezer. Pour the strawberry batter into the pan and smooth with a rubber spatula. Gently spoon the plain layer on top.

7. Place the pan on the center rack of the oven and bake until the cheesecake sets and is lightly brown. If the cake begins to brown too quickly, cover the top loosely with aluminum foil. The cheesecake is done when the center of the cake is firm to the touch.

8. Remove the cake from the oven and place on a wire rack until completely cool (about 2 hours). Once cool, refrigerate for at least 2 hours. When chilled, the cheesecake will come out of the pan easily.

9. Before removing the pan, loosen the cake from the sides with a knife or metal spatula.

10. Spoon the whipped topping into a pastry bag and pipe it decoratively on the cake. Top with sliced strawberries.

11. Cut into wedges and serve.

Raspberries and Cream Cheesecake

INGREDIENT	FOR 6-INCH CAKE	FOR 9-INCH CAKE
Fat-free cream cheese, softened	3 8-ounce packages	6 8-ounce packages
Honey	½ cup	1 cup
Fat-free egg substitute	4 ounces	8 ounces
Nonfat powdered milk	¼ cup mixed with 2 tablespoons water	½ cup mixed with ¼ cup water
Fat-free sour cream	¼ cup	½ cup
Fat-free margarine, melted	¼ cup	½ cup
All-purpose flour	¼ cup	½ cup
Fresh lemon juice	1 tablespoon	2 tablespoons
Vanilla extract	1 teaspoon	2 teaspoons
Puréed raspberries, fresh or frozen*	½ cup	1 cup

CRUST

Graham Cracker (page 8)	single recipe	double recipe

GARNISH

Low-fat whipped topping	1 cup	2 cups
Fresh raspberries	8	16

* Be sure to thaw and drain if using frozen variety.

Baking time	45–60 minutes	1¼–1½ hours
Serves	8	16
Calories per serving	218 (9 from fat)	218 (9 from fat)
Fat per serving	1 gram	1 gram

Fresh, juicy raspberries make this cheesecake something special.

---

1. Preheat the oven to 350°F.

2. Gently pat the prepared crust mixture on the bottom and partially up the sides of a greased springform pan. Place in the freezer for 10 minutes.

3. Blend the cream cheese and honey in an electric mixing bowl or food processor. Add the egg substitute and blend well.

4. Add the powdered milk mixture, sour cream, margarine, and flour, mixing until the batter is smooth and well-combined. Gently stir in the lemon juice and vanilla by hand.

5. Divide the batter in half. Fold the puréed raspberries into one half and leave the other half plain.

6. Remove the springform pan from the freezer. Pour the raspberry batter into the pan and smooth with a rubber spatula. Gently spoon the plain layer on top.

7. Place the pan on the center rack of the oven and bake until the cheesecake sets and is lightly brown. If the cake begins to brown too quickly, cover the top loosely with aluminum foil. The cheesecake is done when the center of the cake is firm to the touch.

8. Remove the cake from the oven and place on a wire rack until completely cool (about 2 hours). Once cool, refrigerate for at least 2 hours. When chilled, the cheesecake will come out of the pan easily.

9. Before removing the pan, loosen the cake from the sides with a knife or metal spatula.

10. Spoon the whipped topping into a pastry bag and pipe rosettes along the top edge. Place a raspberry on each rosette.

11. Cut into wedges and serve.

Blackberries and Cream Cheesecake

INGREDIENT	FOR 6-INCH CAKE	FOR 9-INCH CAKE
Fat-free cream cheese, softened	3 8-ounce packages	6 8-ounce packages
Honey	½ cup	1 cup
Fat-free egg substitute	4 ounces	8 ounces
Nonfat powdered milk	¼ cup mixed with 2 tablespoons water	½ cup mixed with ¼ cup water
Fat-free sour cream	¼ cup	½ cup
Fat-free margarine, melted	¼ cup	½ cup
All-purpose flour	¼ cup	½ cup
Fresh lemon juice	1 tablespoon	2 tablespoons
Vanilla extract	1 teaspoon	2 teaspoons
Puréed blackberries, fresh or frozen*	½ cup	1 cup

CRUST

Graham Cracker (page 8)	single recipe	double recipe

GARNISH

Low-fat whipped topping	1 cup	2 cups
Fresh blackberries	8	16

* Be sure to thaw and drain if using frozen variety.

Baking time	45–60 minutes	1¼–1½ hours
Serves	8	16
Calories per serving	214 (9 from fat)	214 (9 from fat)
Fat per serving	1 gram	1 gram

Layers of luscious blackberries and vanilla cream form a cheesecake that is as eye appealing as it is delicious.

---

1. Preheat the oven to 350°F.

2. Gently pat the prepared crust mixture on the bottom and partially up the sides of a greased springform pan. Place in the freezer for 10 minutes.

3. Blend the cream cheese and honey in an electric mixing bowl or food processor. Add the egg substitute and blend well.

4. Add the powdered milk mixture, sour cream, margarine, and flour, mixing until the batter is smooth and well-combined. Gently stir in the lemon juice and vanilla by hand.

5. Divide the batter in half. Fold the puréed blackberries into one half and leave the other half plain.

6. Remove the springform pan from the freezer. Pour the blackberry batter into the pan and smooth with a rubber spatula. Gently spoon the plain layer on top.

7. Place the pan on the center rack of the oven and bake until the cheesecake sets and is lightly brown. If the cake begins to brown too quickly, cover the top loosely with aluminum foil. The cheesecake is done when the center of the cake is firm to the touch.

8. Remove the cake from the oven and place on a wire rack until completely cool (about 2 hours). Once cool, refrigerate for at least 2 hours. When chilled, the cheesecake will come out of the pan easily.

9. Before removing the pan, loosen the cake from the sides with a knife or metal spatula.

10. Spoon the whipped topping into a pastry bag and pipe rosettes along the top edge of the cake. Place a blackberry on each rosette.

11. Cut into wedges and serve.

Cherries and Cream Cheesecake

INGREDIENT	FOR 6-INCH CAKE	FOR 9-INCH CAKE
Fat-free cream cheese, softened	3 8-ounce packages	6 8-ounce packages
Honey	½ cup	1 cup
Fat-free egg substitute	4 ounces	8 ounces
Nonfat powdered milk	¼ cup mixed with 2 tablespoons water	½ cup mixed with ¼ cup water
Fat-free sour cream	¼ cup	½ cup
Fat-free margarine, melted	¼ cup	½ cup
All-purpose flour	¼ cup	½ cup
Fresh lemon juice	1 tablespoon	2 tablespoons
Vanilla extract	1 teaspoon	2 teaspoons
Puréed dark sweet cherries	½ cup	1 cup
CRUST		
Graham Cracker (page 8)	single recipe	double recipe
GARNISH		
Low-fat whipped topping	1 cup	2 cups
Dark sweet cherries, halved	½ cup	1 cup

Baking time	45–60 minutes	1¼–1½ hours
Serves	8	16
Calories per serving	237 (9 from fat)	237 (9 from fat)
Fat per serving	1 gram	1 gram

Sweet juicy cherries and creamy vanilla make this a cheesecake worth celebrating.

---

1. Preheat the oven to 350°F.

2. Gently pat the prepared crust mixture on the bottom and partially up the sides of a greased springform pan. Place in the freezer for 10 minutes.

3. Blend the cream cheese and honey in an electric mixing bowl or food processor. Add the egg substitute and blend well.

4. Add the powdered milk mixture, sour cream, margarine, and flour, mixing until the batter is smooth and well-combined. Gently stir in the lemon juice and vanilla by hand.

5. Divide the batter in half. Fold the puréed cherries into one half and leave the other half plain.

6. Remove the springform pan from the freezer. Pour the cherry batter into the pan and smooth with a rubber spatula. Gently spoon the plain layer on top.

7. Place the pan on the center rack of the oven and bake until the cheesecake sets and is lightly brown. If the cake begins to brown too quickly, cover the top loosely with aluminum foil. The cheesecake is done when the center of the cake is firm to the touch.

8. Remove the cake from the oven and place on a wire rack until completely cool (about 2 hours). Once cool, refrigerate for at least 2 hours. When chilled, the cheesecake will come out of the pan easily.

9. Before removing the pan, loosen the cake from the sides with a knife or metal spatula.

10. Spoon the whipped topping into a pastry bag and pipe rosettes along the top edge of the cake. Place a cherry half on and between each rosette.

11. Cut into wedges and serve.

Root Beer Float Cheesecake

INGREDIENT	FOR 6-INCH CAKE	FOR 9-INCH CAKE
Fat-free cream cheese, softened	3 8-ounce packages	6 8-ounce packages
Sugar	¾ cup	1½ cups
Fat-free egg substitute	4 ounces	8 ounces
Nonfat powdered milk	¼ cup mixed with 2 tablespoons water	½ cup mixed with ¼ cup water
Fat-free sour cream	¼ cup	½ cup
Fat-free margarine, melted	¼ cup	½ cup
All-purpose flour	¼ cup	½ cup
Fresh lemon juice	1 tablespoon	2 tablespoons
Vanilla extract	1 teaspoon	2 teaspoons
Root beer extract	1 tablespoon	2 tablespoons

CRUST

Graham Cracker (page 8)	single recipe	double recipe

GARNISH

Low-fat whipped topping	1 cup	2 cups
Mini root beer jelly beans	8	16

Baking time	45–60 minutes	1¼–1½ hours
Serves	8	16
Calories per serving	233 (9 from fat)	233 (9 from fat)
Fat per serving	1 gram	1 gram

Root beer float flavor—in a cheesecake.

1. Preheat the oven to 350°F.

2. Gently pat the prepared crust mixture on the bottom and partially up the sides of a greased springform pan. Place in the freezer for 10 minutes.

3. Blend the cream cheese and sugar in an electric mixing bowl or food processor. Add the egg substitute and blend well.

4. Add the powdered milk mixture, sour cream, margarine, and flour, mixing until the batter is smooth and well-combined. Gently stir in the lemon juice and vanilla by hand.

5. Divide the batter in half. Fold the root beer extract into one half and leave the other half plain.

6. Remove the springform pan from the freezer. Pour the root beer batter into the pan and smooth with a rubber spatula. Gently spoon the plain layer on top.

7. Place the pan on the center rack of the oven and bake until the cheesecake sets and is lightly brown. If the cake begins to brown too quickly, cover the top loosely with aluminum foil. The cheesecake is done when the center of the cake is firm to the touch.

8. Remove the cake from the oven and place on a wire rack until completely cool (about 2 hours). Once cool, refrigerate for at least 2 hours. When chilled, the cheesecake will come out of the pan easily.

9. Before removing the pan, loosen the cake from the sides with a knife or metal spatula.

10. Spoon the whipped topping into a pastry bag and pipe rosettes along the top edge of the cake. Place a jelly bean on each rosette.

11. Cut into wedges and serve.

Café au Lait Cheesecake

INGREDIENT	FOR 6-INCH CAKE	FOR 9-INCH CAKE
Fat-free cream cheese, softened	3 8-ounce packages	6 8-ounce packages
Sugar	¾ cup	1½ cups
Fat-free egg substitute	4 ounces	8 ounces
Nonfat powdered milk	¼ cup mixed with 2 tablespoons water	½ cup mixed with ¼ cup water
Fat-free sour cream	¼ cup	½ cup
Fat-free margarine, melted	¼ cup	½ cup
All-purpose flour	¼ cup	½ cup
Fresh lemon juice	1 tablespoon	2 tablespoons
Vanilla extract	1 teaspoon	2 teaspoons
Instant coffee granules	2 teaspoons	4 teaspoons

CRUST

Graham Cracker (page 8)	single recipe	double recipe

GARNISH

Low-fat whipped topping	1 cup	2 cups
Espresso powder	1 teaspoon	2 teaspoons

Baking time	45–60 minutes	1¼–1½ hours
Serves	8	16
Calories per serving	220 (9 from fat)	220 (9 from fat)
Fat per serving	1 gram	1 gram

For a coffee-flavored crust, add 1 teaspoon instant coffee granules to the dough.

---

1. Preheat the oven to 350°F.

2. Gently pat the prepared crust mixture on the bottom and partially up the sides of a greased springform pan. Place in the freezer for 10 minutes.

3. Blend the cream cheese and sugar in an electric mixing bowl or food processor. Add the egg substitute and blend well.

4. Add the powdered milk mixture, sour cream, margarine, and flour, mixing until the batter is smooth and well-combined. Gently stir in the lemon juice and vanilla by hand.

5. Divide the batter in half. Fold the coffee granules into one half and leave the other half plain.

6. Remove the springform pan from the freezer. Pour the coffee batter into the pan and smooth with a rubber spatula. Gently spoon the plain layer on top.

7. Place the pan on the center rack of the oven and bake until the cheesecake sets and is lightly brown. If the cake begins to brown too quickly, cover the top loosely with aluminum foil. The cheesecake is done when the center of the cake is firm to the touch.

8. Remove the cake from the oven and place on a wire rack until completely cool (about 2 hours). Once cool, refrigerate for at least 2 hours. When chilled, the cheesecake will come out of the pan easily.

9. Before removing the pan, loosen the cake from the sides with a knife or metal spatula.

10. Dust the cake with espresso powder and pipe on topping.

11. Cut into wedges and serve.

Amaretto and Cream Cheesecake

INGREDIENT	FOR 6-INCH CAKE	FOR 9-INCH CAKE
Fat-free cream cheese, softened	3 8-ounce packages	6 8-ounce packages
Sugar	¾ cup	1½ cups
Fat-free egg substitute	4 ounces	8 ounces
Nonfat powdered milk	¼ cup mixed with 2 tablespoons water	½ cup mixed with ¼ cup water
Fat-free sour cream	¼ cup	½ cup
Fat-free margarine, melted	¼ cup	½ cup
All-purpose flour	¼ cup	½ cup
Fresh lemon juice	1 tablespoon	2 tablespoons
Vanilla extract	1 teaspoon	2 teaspoons
Amaretto liqueur	¼ cup	½ cup

CRUST

Graham Cracker (page 8)	single recipe	double recipe

GARNISH

Low-fat whipped topping	1 cup	2 cups
Sliced almonds	1 teaspoon	2 teaspoons

Baking time	45–60 minutes	1¼–1 ½ hours
Serves	8	16
Calories per serving	274 (9 from fat)	274 (9 from fat)
Fat per serving	1 gram	1 gram

This delicate almond-flavored cheesecake makes an elegant dessert.

---

1. Preheat the oven to 350°F.

2. Gently pat the prepared crust mixture on the bottom and partially up the sides of a greased springform pan. Place in the freezer for 10 minutes.

3. Blend the cream cheese and sugar in an electric mixing bowl or food processor. Add the egg substitute and blend well.

4. Add the powdered milk mixture, sour cream, margarine, and flour, mixing until the batter is smooth and well-combined. Gently stir in the lemon juice and vanilla by hand.

5. Divide the batter in half. Stir the amaretto into one half and leave the other half plain.

6. Remove the springform pan from the freezer. Pour the amaretto batter into the pan and smooth with a rubber spatula. Gently spoon the plain layer on top.

7. Place the pan on the center rack of the oven and bake until the cheesecake sets and is lightly brown. If the cake begins to brown too quickly, cover the top loosely with aluminum foil. The cheesecake is done when the center of the cake is firm to the touch.

8. Remove the cake from the oven and place on a wire rack until completely cool (about 2 hours). Once cool, refrigerate for at least 2 hours. When chilled, the cheesecake will come out of the pan easily.

9. Before removing the pan, loosen the cake from the sides with a knife or metal spatula.

10. Spoon the topping into a pastry bag and pipe it decoratively on the cake. Top with a sprinkling of almonds.

11. Cut into wedges and serve.

Orange Creamsicle Cheesecake

INGREDIENT	FOR 6-INCH CAKE	FOR 9-INCH CAKE
Fat-free cream cheese, softened	3 8-ounce packages	6 8-ounce packages
Sugar	¾ cup	1 ½ cups
Fat-free egg substitute	4 ounces	8 ounces
Nonfat powdered milk	¼ cup mixed with 2 tablespoons water	½ cup mixed with ¼ cup water
Fat-free sour cream	¼ cup	½ cup
Fat-free margarine, melted	¼ cup	½ cup
All-purpose flour	¼ cup	½ cup
Fresh lemon juice	1 tablespoon	2 tablespoons
Vanilla extract	1 teaspoon	2 teaspoons
Puréed seedless oranges or orange juice concentrate	½ cup	1 cup

CRUST

Zesty Orange Graham Cracker (page 12)	single recipe	double recipe

GARNISH

Low-fat whipped topping	1 cup	2 cups
Orange segments	8	16

Baking time	45–60 minutes	1 ¼–1 ½ hours
Serves	8	16
Calories per serving	221 (9 from fat)	221 (9 from fat)
Fat per serving	1 gram	1 gram

Cool orange and creamy vanilla—the perfect summer treat.

---

1. Preheat the oven to 350°F.

2. Gently pat the prepared crust mixture on the bottom and partially up the sides of a greased springform pan. Place in the freezer for 10 minutes.

3. Blend the cream cheese and sugar in an electric mixing bowl or food processor. Add the egg substitute and blend well.

4. Add the powdered milk mixture, sour cream, margarine, and flour, mixing until the batter is smooth and well-combined. Gently stir in the lemon juice and vanilla by hand.

5. Divide the batter in half. Fold the puréed oranges into one half and leave the other half plain.

6. Remove the springform pan from the freezer. Pour the orange batter into the pan and smooth with a rubber spatula. Gently spoon the plain layer on top.

7. Place the pan on the center rack of the oven and bake until the cheesecake sets and is lightly brown. If the cake begins to brown too quickly, cover the top loosely with aluminum foil. The cheesecake is done when the center of the cake is firm to the touch.

8. Remove the cake from the oven and place on a wire rack until completely cool (about 2 hours). Once cool, refrigerate for at least 2 hours. When chilled, the cheesecake will come out of the pan easily.

9. Before removing the pan, loosen the cake from the sides with a knife or metal spatula.

10. Arrange the orange segments in a circle in the center of the cake. Pipe the whipped topping decoratively along the top edge.

11. Cut into wedges and serve.

Variation

Use puréed tangerines instead of oranges for another delicious version of this cake.

Grapes and Cream Cheesecake

INGREDIENT	FOR 6-INCH CAKE	FOR 9-INCH CAKE
Fat-free cream cheese, softened	3 8-ounce packages	6 8-ounce packages
Sugar	¾ cup	1½ cups
Fat-free egg substitute	4 ounces	8 ounces
Nonfat powdered milk	¼ cup mixed with 2 tablespoons water	½ cup mixed with ¼ cup water
Fat-free sour cream	¼ cup	½ cup
Fat-free margarine, melted	¼ cup	½ cup
All-purpose flour	¼ cup	½ cup
Fresh lemon juice	1 tablespoon	2 tablespoons
Vanilla extract	1 teaspoon	2 teaspoons
Purple grape juice concentrate	½ cup	1 cup

CRUST

Graham Cracker (page 8)	single recipe	double recipe

GARNISH

Low-fat whipped topping	1 cup	2 cups
Fresh grapes	8	16

Baking time	45–60 minutes	1¼–1½ hours
Serves	8	16
Calories per serving	238 (9 from fat)	238 (9 from fat)
Fat per serving	1 gram	1 gram

Here's one for the kids (or for the kid in you).

---

1. Preheat the oven to 350°F.

2. Gently pat the prepared crust mixture on the bottom and partially up the sides of a greased springform pan. Place in the freezer for 10 minutes.

3. Blend the cream cheese and sugar in an electric mixing bowl or food processor. Add the egg substitute and blend well.

4. Add the powdered milk mixture, sour cream, margarine, and flour, mixing until the batter is smooth and well-combined. Gently stir in the lemon juice and vanilla by hand.

5. Divide the batter in half. Stir the grape juice into one half and leave the other half plain.

6. Remove the springform pan from the freezer. Pour the grape batter into the pan and smooth with a rubber spatula. Gently spoon the plain layer on top.

7. Place the pan on the center rack of the oven and bake until the cheesecake sets and is lightly brown. If the cake begins to brown too quickly, cover the top loosely with aluminum foil. The cheesecake is done when the center of the cake is firm to the touch.

8. Remove the cake from the oven and place on a wire rack until completely cool (about 2 hours). Once cool, refrigerate for at least 2 hours. When chilled, the cheesecake will come out of the pan easily.

9. Before removing the pan, loosen the cake from the sides with a knife or metal spatula.

10. Spoon the whipped topping into a pastry bag and pipe rosettes along the edge of the cake. Place a grape on each rosette.

11. Cut into wedges and serve.

Melons and Cream Cheesecake

INGREDIENT	FOR 6-INCH CAKE	FOR 9-INCH CAKE
Fat-free cream cheese, softened	3 8-ounce packages	6 8-ounce packages
Sugar	¾ cup	1½ cups
Fat-free egg substitute	4 ounces	8 ounces
Nonfat powdered milk	¼ cup mixed with 2 tablespoons water	½ cup mixed with ¼ cup water
Fat-free sour cream	¼ cup	½ cup
Fat-free margarine, melted	¼ cup	½ cup
All-purpose flour	¼ cup	½ cup
Fresh lemon juice	1 tablespoon	2 tablespoons
Vanilla extract	1 teaspoon	2 teaspoons
Puréed honeydew melon, drained	½ cup	1 cup

CRUST

Graham Cracker (page 8)	single recipe	double recipe

GARNISH

Low-fat whipped topping	1 cup	2 cups
Thin honeydew wedges	8 (¼ honeydew)	16 (½ honeydew)

Baking time	45–60 minutes	1¼–1½ hours
Serves	8	16
Calories per serving	223 (9 from fat)	223 (9 from fat)
Fat per serving	1 gram	1 gram

This cheesecake spotlights the light delicate flavor and color of honeydew melon.

---

1. Preheat the oven to 350°F.

2. Gently pat the prepared crust mixture on the bottom and partially up the sides of a greased springform pan. Place in the freezer for 10 minutes.

3. Blend the cream cheese and sugar in an electric mixing bowl or food processor. Add the egg substitute and blend well.

4. Add the powdered milk mixture, sour cream, margarine, and flour, mixing until the batter is smooth and well-combined. Gently stir in the lemon juice and vanilla by hand.

5. Divide the batter in half. Fold the puréed honeydew into one half and leave the other half plain.

6. Remove the springform pan from the freezer. Pour the honeydew batter into the pan and smooth with a rubber spatula. Gently spoon the plain layer on top.

7. Place the pan on the center rack of the oven and bake until the cheesecake sets and is lightly brown. If the cake begins to brown too quickly, cover the top loosely with aluminum foil. The cheesecake is done when the center of the cake is firm to the touch.

8. Remove the cake from the oven and place on a wire rack until completely cool (about 2 hours). Once cool, refrigerate for at least 2 hours. When chilled, the cheesecake will come out of the pan easily.

9. Before removing the pan, loosen the cake from the sides with a knife or metal spatula.

10. Arrange the honeydew slices in a circle on the center of the cake. Pipe the whipped topping decoratively along the top edge.

11. Cut into wedges and serve.

Variation

Use puréed mango instead of honeydew for another yummy variation of this recipe.

Pineapple with Coconut Cream

INGREDIENT	FOR 6-INCH CAKE	FOR 9-INCH CAKE
Fat-free cream cheese, softened	3 8-ounce packages	6 8-ounce packages
Sugar	¾ cup	1½ cups
Fat-free egg substitute	4 ounces	8 ounces
Nonfat powdered milk	¼ cup mixed with 2 tablespoons water	½ cup mixed with ¼ cup water
Fat-free sour cream	¼ cup	½ cup
Fat-free margarine, melted	¼ cup	½ cup
All-purpose flour	¼ cup	½ cup
Fresh lemon juice	1 tablespoon	2 tablespoons
Vanilla extract	1 teaspoon	2 teaspoons
Puréed pineapple, fresh or canned*	½ cup	1 cup
Coconut extract	1 teaspoon	2 teaspoons

CRUST

Coconut Graham Cracker (page 20)	single recipe	double recipe

GARNISH

Low-fat whipped topping	1 cup	2 cups
Pineapple rings, halved	4	8

* Be sure to drain if using canned variety.

Baking time	45–60 minutes	1¼–1½ hours
Serves	8	16
Calories per serving	240 (9 from fat)	240 (9 from fat)
Fat per serving	1 gram	1 gram

Layers of pineapple and coconut give this yummy cheesecake a tropical twist.

---

1. Preheat the oven to 350°F.

2. Gently pat the prepared crust mixture on the bottom and partially up the sides of a greased springform pan. Place in the freezer for 10 minutes.

3. Blend the cream cheese and sugar in an electric mixing bowl or food processor. Add the egg substitute and blend well.

4. Add the powdered milk mixture, sour cream, margarine, and flour, mixing until the batter is smooth and well-combined. Gently stir in the lemon juice and vanilla by hand.

5. Divide the batter in half. Fold the puréed pineapple into one half and stir the coconut extract into the other.

6. Remove the springform pan from the freezer. Pour the pineapple batter into the pan and smooth with a rubber spatula. Gently spoon the coconut layer on top.

7. Place the pan on the center rack of the oven and bake until the cheesecake sets and is lightly brown. If the cake begins to brown too quickly, cover the top loosely with aluminum foil. The cheesecake is done when the center of the cake is firm to the touch.

8. Remove the cake from the oven and place on a wire rack until completely cool (about 2 hours). Once cool, refrigerate for at least 2 hours. When chilled, the cheesecake will come out of the pan easily.

9. Before removing the pan, loosen the cake from the sides with a knife or metal spatula.

10. Spoon the whipped topping into a pastry bag and pipe it decoratively on the cake. Top with pineapple slices.

11. Cut into wedges and serve.

Lemon and Cream Cheesecake

INGREDIENT	FOR 6-INCH CAKE	FOR 9-INCH CAKE
Fat-free cream cheese, softened	3 8-ounce packages	6 8-ounce packages
Sugar	¾ cup	1½ cups
Fat-free egg substitute	4 ounces	8 ounces
Nonfat powdered milk	¼ cup mixed with 2 tablespoons water	½ cup mixed with ¼ cup water
Fat-free sour cream	¼ cup	½ cup
Fat-free margarine, melted	¼ cup	½ cup
All-purpose flour	¼ cup	½ cup
Vanilla extract	1 teaspoon	2 teaspoons
Fresh lemon juice	⅓ cup	⅔ cup
Yellow food coloring	2 drops	4 drops

CRUST

Lemon Graham Cracker (page 14)	single recipe	double recipe

GARNISH

Low-fat whipped topping	1 cup	2 cups
Grated lemon zest	1 tablespoon	2 tablespoons

Baking time	45–60 minutes	1¼–1½ hours
Serves	8	16
Calories per serving	223 (9 from fat)	223 (9 from fat)
Fat per serving	1 gram	1 gram

The perfect treat to serve on a hot summer day

---

1. Preheat the oven to 350°F.

2. Gently pat the prepared crust mixture on the bottom and partially up the sides of a greased springform pan. Place in the freezer for 10 minutes.

3. Blend the cream cheese and sugar in an electric mixing bowl or food processor. Add the egg substitute and blend well.

4. Add the powdered milk mixture, sour cream, margarine, and flour, mixing until the batter is smooth and well-combined. Gently stir in the vanilla by hand.

5. Divide the batter in half. Stir the lemon juice and the yellow food coloring into one half and leave the other half plain.

6. Remove the springform pan from the freezer. Pour the lemon batter into the pan and smooth with a rubber spatula. Gently spoon the plain layer on top.

7. Place the pan on the center rack of the oven and bake until the cheesecake sets and is lightly brown. If the cake begins to brown too quickly, cover the top loosely with aluminum foil. The cheesecake is done when the center of the cake is firm to the touch.

8. Remove the cake from the oven and place on a wire rack until completely cool (about 2 hours). Once cool, refrigerate for at least 2 hours. When chilled, the cheesecake will come out of the pan easily.

9. Before removing the pan, loosen the cake from the sides with a knife or metal spatula.

10. Spoon the whipped topping decoratively on top of the cake and sprinkle with lemon zest.

11. Cut into wedges and serve.

Variations

For a lime version of this cake, use lime juice and green food coloring, instead of the lemon and prepare in a Zesty Lime Oat Crust (page 28). For a lemon-lime version, layer the two flavors and prepare in the lemon or lime crust of your choice.

Butterscotch and Cream Cheesecake

INGREDIENT	FOR 6-INCH CAKE	FOR 9-INCH CAKE
Fat-free cream cheese, softened	3 8-ounce packages	6 8-ounce packages
Sugar	¾ cup	1½ cups
Fat-free egg substitute	4 ounces	8 ounces
Nonfat powdered milk	¼ cup mixed with 2 tablespoons water	½ cup mixed with ¼ cup water
Fat-free sour cream	¼ cup	½ cup
Fat-free margarine, melted	¼ cup	½ cup
All-purpose flour	¼ cup	½ cup
Fresh lemon juice	1 tablespoon	2 tablespoons
Vanilla extract	1 teaspoon	2 teaspoons
Fat-free butterscotch ice cream topping	½ cup	1 cup

CRUST		
Graham Cracker (page 8)	single recipe	double recipe

GARNISH		
Low-fat whipped topping	1 cup	2 cups
Crushed butterscotch candy	2 tablespoons	¼ cup

Baking time	45–60 minutes	1¼–1½ hours
Serves	8	16
Calories per serving	257 (9 from fat)	257 (9 from fat)
Fat per serving	1 gram	1 gram

Layers of butterscotch and vanilla combine for a rich, creamy treat.

---

1. Preheat the oven to 350°F.

2. Gently pat the prepared crust mixture on the bottom and partially up the sides of a greased springform pan. Place in the freezer for 10 minutes.

3. Blend the cream cheese and sugar in an electric mixing bowl or food processor. Add the egg substitute and blend well.

4. Add the powdered milk mixture, sour cream, margarine, and flour, mixing until the batter is smooth and well-combined. Gently stir in the lemon juice and vanilla by hand.

5. Divide the batter in half. Fold the butterscotch into one half and leave the other half plain.

6. Remove the springform pan from the freezer. Pour the butterscotch batter into the pan and smooth with a rubber spatula. Gently spoon the plain layer on top.

7. Place the pan on the center rack of the oven and bake until the cheesecake sets and is lightly brown. If the cake begins to brown too quickly, cover the top loosely with aluminum foil. The cheesecake is done when the center of the cake is firm to the touch.

8. Remove the cake from the oven and place on a wire rack until completely cool (about 2 hours). Once cool, refrigerate for at least 2 hours. When chilled, the cheesecake will come out of the pan easily.

9. Before removing the pan, loosen the cake from the sides with a knife or metal spatula.

10. Spoon the whipped topping on the cake and sprinkle with crushed butterscotch candy.

11. Cut into wedges and serve.

Variation

For a creamy caramel version, use fat-free caramel ice cream topping instead of butterscotch.

Pumpkin and Cream Cheesecake

INGREDIENT	FOR 6-INCH CAKE	FOR 9-INCH CAKE
Fat-free cream cheese, softened	3 8-ounce packages	6 8-ounce packages
Honey	½ cup	1 cup
Fat-free egg substitute	4 ounces	8 ounces
Nonfat powdered milk	¼ cup mixed with 2 tablespoons water	½ cup mixed with ¼ cup water
Fat-free sour cream	¼ cup	½ cup
Fat-free margarine, melted	¼ cup	½ cup
All-purpose flour	¼ cup	½ cup
Fresh lemon juice	1 tablespoon	2 tablespoons
Vanilla extract	1 teaspoon	2 teaspoons
Canned pumpkin	½ cup	1 cup
Pumpkin pie spice	1 teaspoon	2 teaspoons

CRUST

Graham Cracker (page 8)	single recipe	double recipe

GARNISH

Low-fat whipped topping	1 cup	2 cups
Nutmeg	1 teaspoon	2 teaspoons

Baking time	45–60 minutes	1¼–1½ hours
Serves	8	16
Calories per serving	211 (9 from fat)	211 (9 from fat)
Fat per serving	1 gram	1 gram

The pumpkin in this cheesecake adds fiber as well as great flavor.

---

1. Preheat the oven to 350°F.

2. Gently pat the prepared crust mixture on the bottom and partially up the sides of a greased springform pan. Place in the freezer for 10 minutes.

3. Blend the cream cheese and honey in an electric mixing bowl or food processor. Add the egg substitute and blend well.

4. Add the powdered milk mixture, sour cream, margarine, and flour, mixing until the batter is smooth and well-combined. Gently stir in the lemon juice and vanilla by hand.

5. Divide the batter in half. Fold the pumpkin and pumpkin spice into one half and leave the other half plain.

6. Remove the springform pan from the freezer. Pour the orange batter into the pan and smooth with a rubber spatula. Gently spoon the plain layer on top.

7. Place the pan on the center rack of the oven and bake until the cheesecake sets and is lightly brown. If the cake begins to brown too quickly, cover the top loosely with aluminum foil. The cheesecake is done when the center of the cake is firm to the touch.

8. Remove the cake from the oven and place on a wire rack until completely cool (about 2 hours). Once cool, refrigerate for at least 2 hours. When chilled, the cheesecake will come out of the pan easily.

9. Before removing the pan, loosen the cake from the sides with a knife or metal spatula.

10. Pipe the whipped topping decoratively on top and dust with nutmeg.

11. Cut into wedges and serve.

Roses and Cream Cheesecake

INGREDIENT	FOR 6-INCH CAKE	FOR 9-INCH CAKE
Fat-free cream cheese, softened	3 8-ounce packages	6 8-ounce packages
Sugar	¾ cup	1½ cups
Fat-free egg substitute	4 ounces	8 ounces
Nonfat powdered milk	¼ cup mixed with 2 tablespoons water	½ cup mixed with ¼ cup water
Fat-free sour cream	¼ cup	½ cup
Fat-free margarine, melted	¼ cup	½ cup
All-purpose flour	¼ cup	½ cup
Fresh lemon juice	1 tablespoon	2 tablespoons
Vanilla extract	1 teaspoon	2 teaspoons
Rose syrup*	½ cup	1 cup
Red food coloring	2 drop	4 drops
CRUST		
Graham Cracker (page 8)	single recipe	double recipe
GARNISH		
Low-fat whipped topping	1 cup	2 cups
Pink or red rosebuds	1 or 2	2 or 3

* Rose syrup is available in Greek and Middle Eastern markets. To make your own, see recipe on page 154.

Baking time	45–60 minutes	1¼–1½ hours
Serves	8	16
Calories per serving	237 (9 from fat)	237 (9 from fat)
Fat per serving	1 gram	1 gram

This cheesecake, with its delicate rose and rich vanilla flavors is simply elegant.

---

1. Preheat the oven to 350°F.

2. Gently pat the prepared crust mixture on the bottom and partially up the sides of a greased springform pan. Place in the freezer for 10 minutes.

3. Blend the cream cheese and sugar in an electric mixing bowl or food processor. Add the egg substitute and blend well.

4. Add the powdered milk mixture, sour cream, margarine, and flour, mixing until the batter is smooth and well-combined. Gently stir in the lemon juice and vanilla by hand.

5. Divide the batter in half. Stir the rose syrup and food coloring into one half and leave the other half plain.

6. Remove the springform pan from the freezer. Pour the rose batter into the pan and smooth with a rubber spatula. Gently spoon the plain layer on top.

7. Place the pan on the center rack of the oven and bake until the cheesecake sets and is lightly brown. If the cake begins to brown too quickly, cover the top loosely with aluminum foil. The cheesecake is done when the center of the cake is firm to the touch.

8. Remove the cake from the oven and place on a wire rack until completely cool (about 2 hours). Once cool, refrigerate for at least 2 hours. When chilled, the cheesecake will come out of the pan easily.

9. Before removing the pan, loosen the cake from the sides with a knife or metal spatula.

10. Arrange the rosebuds in the center of the cake and pipe the whipped topping in rosettes along the edge.

11. Cut into wedges and serve.

Mango–Berry Cheesecake

INGREDIENT	FOR 6-INCH CAKE	FOR 9-INCH CAKE
Fat-free cream cheese, softened	2 8-ounce packages	4 8-ounce packages
Firm tofu, mashed	8 ounces	16 ounces
Honey	½ cup	1 cup
Fat-free egg substitute	4 ounces	8 ounces
Nonfat powdered milk	¼ cup mixed with 2 tablespoons water	½ cup mixed with ¼ cup water
Fat-free sour cream	¼ cup	½ cup
Fat-free yogurt	¼ cup	½ cup
Fresh lemon juice	1 tablespoon	2 tablespoons
Vanilla extract	1 teaspoon	2 teaspoons
Puréed mango	½ cup	1 cup
Puréed strawberries or raspberries, fresh or frozen*	½ cup	1 cup

CRUST

Graham Cracker (page 8)	single recipe	double recipe

GARNISH

Low-fat whipped topping	1 cup	2 cups
Fresh strawberries or raspberries	1 cup	2 cups

* Be sure to thaw and drain if using frozen variety.

Baking time	45–60 minutes	1¼–1½ hours
Serves	8	16
Calories per serving	228 (25 from fat)	228 (25 from fat)
Fat per serving	2.75 grams	2.75 grams

Cool mangoes and juicy berries are a flavorful combination in this visually appealing cheesecake.

---

1. Preheat the oven to 350°F.

2. Gently pat the prepared crust mixture on the bottom and partially up the sides of a greased springform pan. Place in the freezer for 10 minutes.

3. Blend the cream cheese and sugar in an electric mixing bowl or food processor. Add the egg substitute and blend well.

4. Add the powdered milk mixture, sour cream, and yogurt, mixing until the batter is smooth and well-combined. Gently stir in the lemon juice and vanilla by hand.

5. Divide the batter in half. Fold the puréed mangoes into one half and the puréed berries into the other.

6. Remove the springform pan from the freezer. Pour the berry batter into the pan and smooth with a rubber spatula. Gently spoon the mango layer on top.

7. Place the pan on the center rack of the oven and bake until the cheesecake sets and is lightly brown. If the cake begins to brown too quickly, cover the top loosely with aluminum foil. The cheesecake is done when the center of the cake is firm to the touch.

8. Remove the cake from the oven and place on a wire rack until completely cool (about 2 hours). Once cool, refrigerate for at least 2 hours. When chilled, the cheesecake will come out of the pan easily.

9. Before removing the pan, loosen the cake from the sides with a knife or metal spatula.

10. Spoon the whipped topping on the cake and decorate with fresh berries.

11. Cut into wedges and serve.

Lemon–Raspberry Cheesecake

INGREDIENT	FOR 6-INCH CAKE	FOR 9-INCH CAKE
Fat-free cream cheese, softened	2 8-ounce packages	4 8-ounce packages
Firm tofu, mashed	8 ounces	16 ounces
Honey	½ cup	1 cup
Fat-free egg substitute	4 ounces	8 ounces
Nonfat powdered milk	¼ cup mixed with 2 tablespoons water	½ cup mixed with ¼ cup water
Fat-free sour cream	¼ cup	½ cup
Fat-free yogurt	¼ cup	½ cup
Vanilla extract	1 teaspoon	2 teaspoons
Puréed raspberries, fresh or frozen*	½ cup	1 cup
Fresh lemon juice	⅓ cup	⅔ cup
Yellow food coloring	2 drops	4 drops
CRUST		
Graham Cracker (page 8)	single recipe	double recipe
GARNISH		
Low-fat whipped topping	1 cup	2 cups
Fresh raspberries	½ cup	1 cup
Grated lemon zest	1 tablespoon	2 tablespoons

* Be sure to thaw and drain if using frozen variety.

Baking time	45–60 minutes	1¼–1½ hours
Serves	8	16
Calories per serving	222 (25 from fat)	222 (25 from fat)
Fat per serving	2.75 gram	2.75 grams

These two flavors combine to form one of my most popular cheesecakes.

---

1. Preheat the oven to 350°F.

2. Gently pat the prepared crust mixture on the bottom and partially up the sides of a greased springform pan. Place in the freezer for 10 minutes.

3. Blend the cream cheese and honey in an electric mixing bowl or food processor. Add the egg substitute and blend well.

4. Add the powdered milk mixture, sour cream, and yogurt, mixing until the batter is smooth and well-combined. Gently stir in the vanilla by hand.

5. Divide the batter in half. Fold the puréed raspberries into one half, and the lemon juice and food coloring into the other.

6. Remove the springform pan from the freezer. Pour the raspberry batter into the pan and smooth with a rubber spatula. Gently spoon the lemon layer on top.

7. Place the pan on the center rack of the oven and bake until the cheesecake sets and is lightly brown. If the cake begins to brown too quickly, cover the top loosely with aluminum foil. The cheesecake is done when the center of the cake is firm to the touch.

8. Remove the cake from the oven and place on a wire rack until completely cool (about 2 hours). Once cool, refrigerate for at least 2 hours. When chilled, the cheesecake will come out of the pan easily.

9. Before removing the pan, loosen the cake from the sides with a knife or metal spatula.

10. Spoon the whipped topping on the cake and decorate with fresh raspberries and lemon zest.

11. Cut into wedges and serve.

Cherry–Tangerine Cheesecake

INGREDIENT	FOR 6-INCH CAKE	FOR 9-INCH CAKE
Fat-free cream cheese, softened	2 8-ounce packages	4 8-ounce packages
Firm tofu, mashed	8 ounces	16 ounces
Honey	½ cup	1 cup
Fat-free egg substitute	4 ounces	8 ounces
Nonfat powdered milk	¼ cup mixed with 2 tablespoons water	½ cup mixed with ¼ cup water
Fat-free sour cream	¼ cup	½ cup
Fat-free yogurt	¼ cup	½ cup
Fresh lemon juice	1 tablespoon	2 tablespoons
Vanilla extract	1 teaspoon	2 teaspoons
Puréed dark sweet cherries	½ cup	1 cup
Puréed tangerines	½ cup	1 cup
CRUST		
Graham Cracker (page 8)	single recipe	double recipe
GARNISH		
Low-fat whipped topping	1 cup	2 cups
Dark sweet cherries	½ cup	1 cup
Grated tangerine zest	1 tablespoon	2 tablespoons

Baking time	45–60 minutes	1¼–1½ hours
Serves	8	16
Calories per serving	231 (25 from fat)	231 (25 from fat)
Fat per serving	2.75 grams	2.75 grams

This cheesecake is beautiful and delicious.

---

1. Preheat the oven to 350°F.

2. Gently pat the prepared crust mixture on the bottom and partially up the sides of a greased springform pan. Place in the freezer for 10 minutes.

3. Blend the cream cheese and honey in an electric mixing bowl or food processor. Add the egg substitute and blend well.

4. Add the powdered milk mixture, sour cream, and yogurt, mixing until the batter is smooth and well-combined. Gently stir in the lemon juice and vanilla by hand.

5. Divide the batter in half. Fold the puréed cherries into one half, and the puréed tangerines into the other.

6. Remove the springform pan from the freezer. Pour the cherry batter into the pan and smooth with a rubber spatula. Gently spoon the tangerine layer on top.

7. Place the pan on the center rack of the oven and bake until the cheesecake sets and is lightly brown. If the cake begins to brown too quickly, cover the top loosely with aluminum foil. The cheesecake is done when the center of the cake is firm to the touch.

8. Remove the cake from the oven and place on a wire rack until completely cool (about 2 hours). Once cool, refrigerate for at least 2 hours. When chilled, the cheesecake will come out of the pan easily.

9. Before removing the pan, loosen the cake from the sides with a knife or metal spatula.

10. Spoon the whipped topping on the cake and decorate with cherries and tangerine zest.

11. Cut into wedges and serve.

Top: No-Bake Peppermint
Cheesecake (page 252)

Center: Peanut Butter Cup
Cheesecake (page 164)

Bottom: Cookies-and-Cream
Cheesecake (page 150)

Top: **Perfect Pumpkin Cheesecake** *(page 134)*

Left: **Creamy Eggnog Cheesecake** *(page 132)*

Right: **Rum Raisin Cheesecake** *(page 138)*

9.

No-Bake Cheesecake Classics

If you don't have time to bake, but still crave rich and creamy cheesecake desserts, this is the chapter for you. In it you will find a generous variety of no-bake cheesecakes ranging from the simple and basic to the tantalizingly exotic.

Unlike the other cakes in this book, the no-bake cheesecakes are not prepared in springform pans. Rather they are made in 8-inch pie pans that serve eight. Instructions for doubling the recipes are also provided.

Because these cheesecakes are rich and creamy enough by themselves, they don't need added whipped topping as a garnish. Of course, this decision is entirely up to you. I have also given you the option of including a few jelly beans in a number of fillings just for fun. I find that they bring an added fat-free dimension to the cakes.

If you like the idea of no-bake cheesecakes, you're going to love preparing and serving the following desserts. And be sure to take a look at the beautiful no-bake layered creations in Chapter 10.

Basic No-Bake Cheesecake

INGREDIENT	ONE 8-INCH CAKE	TWO 8-INCH CAKES
Fat-free cream cheese, softened	2 8-ounce packages	4 8-ounce packages
Sugar	¾ cup	1½ cups
Low-fat whipped topping	½ cup	1 cup
Fat-free yogurt	¼ cup	½ cup
Fat-free sour cream	¼ cup	½ cup
Vanilla extract	1 teaspoon	2 teaspoons
Fresh lemon juice	½ teaspoon	1 teaspoon
Unflavored gelatin	1 tablespoon mixed with 1 tablespoon water	2 tablespoons mixed with 2 tablespoons water

CRUST		
Graham Cracker (page 8)	single recipe	double recipe

Chilling time	2 hours	2 hours
Serves	8	16
Calories per serving	171 (9 from fat)	171 (9 from fat)
Fat per serving	1 gram	1 gram

Not only is this cheesecake quick and easy to make—it's practically fat-free!

---

1. Gently pat the prepared crust mixture on the bottom and sides of an 8-inch pie plate (or plates).

2. Blend together the cream cheese and sugar with an electric mixer. Add the whipped topping, yogurt, sour cream, vanilla, and lemon juice. Continue to blend until smooth and well-combined.

3. Drizzle the gelatin over the mixture and fold in gently.

4. Pour the batter into the prepared crust (or crusts) and smooth with a spatula. Cover with plastic wrap and refrigerate at least 2 hours.

5. Cut into wedges and serve.

Basic No-Bake
Tofu Cheesecake

INGREDIENT	ONE 8-INCH CAKE	TWO 8-INCH CAKES
Fat-free cream cheese, softened	1 8-ounce package	2 8-ounce packages
Tofu, mashed	8 ounces	16 ounces
Sugar	¾ cup	1½ cups
Low-fat whipped topping	½ cup	1 cup
Fat-free yogurt	¼ cup	½ cup
Fat-free sour cream	¼ cup	½ cup
Vanilla extract	1 teaspoon	2 teaspoons
Fresh lemon juice	½ teaspoon	1 teaspoon
Unflavored gelatin	1 tablespoon mixed with 1 tablespoon water	2 tablespoons mixed with 2 tablespoons water

CRUST

Graham Cracker (page 8)	single recipe	double recipe

Chilling time	2 hours	2 hours
Serves	8	16
Calories per serving	188 (25 from fat)	188 (25 from fat)
Fat per serving	2.75 grams	2.75 grams

To ensure the tofu is fresh be sure to check its expiration date.

---

1. Gently pat the prepared crust mixture on the bottom and sides of an 8-inch pie plate (or plates).

2. Blend together the cream cheese, tofu, and sugar with an electric mixer. Add the whipped topping, yogurt, sour cream, vanilla, and lemon juice. Continue to blend until smooth and well-combined.

3. Drizzle the gelatin over the mixture and fold in gently.

4. Pour the batter into the prepared crust (or crusts) and smooth with a spatula. Cover with plastic wrap and refrigerate at least 2 hours.

5. Cut into wedges and serve.

Basic No-Bake Ricotta Cheesecake

INGREDIENT	ONE 8-INCH CAKE	TWO 8-INCH CAKES
Fat-free ricotta cheese	1 pound	2 pounds
Sugar	¾ cup	1½ cups
Low-fat whipped topping	½ cup	1 cup
Fat-free yogurt	¼ cup	½ cup
Fat-free sour cream	¼ cup	½ cup
Vanilla extract	1 teaspoon	2 teaspoons
Fresh lemon juice	½ teaspoon	1 teaspoon
Unflavored gelatin	1 tablespoon mixed with 1 tablespoon water	2 tablespoons mixed with 2 tablespoons water
CRUST		
Graham Cracker (page 8)	single recipe	double recipe

Chilling time	2 hours	2 hours
Serves	8	16
Calories per serving	192 (9 from fat)	192 (9 from fat)
Fat per serving	1 gram	1 gram

This ricotta cheesecake is light and creamy and oh-so easy to prepare.

---

1. Gently pat the prepared crust mixture on the bottom and sides of an 8-inch pie plate (or plates).

2. Blend together the ricotta cheese, tofu, and sugar with an electric mixer. Add the whipped topping, yogurt, sour cream, vanilla, and lemon juice. Continue to blend until smooth and well-combined.

3. Drizzle the gelatin over the mixture and fold in gently.

4. Pour the batter into the prepared crust (or crusts) and smooth with a spatula. Cover with plastic wrap and refrigerate at least 2 hours.

5. Cut into wedges and serve.

Basic No-Bake Lactose-Free Cheesecake

INGREDIENT	ONE 8-INCH CAKE	TWO 8-INCH CAKES
Tofu, mashed	1 cup	2 cups
Tahini*	½ cup	1 cup
Chick peas, drained and mashed	½ cup	1 cup
Sugar	¾ cup	1½ cups
Soy milk	½ cup	1 cup
Fresh lemon juice	1 tablespoon	2 tablespoons
Vanilla extract	1 teaspoon	2 teaspoons
Unflavored gelatin	1 tablespoon mixed with 1 tablespoon water	2 tablespoons mixed with 2 tablespoons water

CRUST

Graham Cracker (page 8)	single recipe	double recipe

* Tahini (puréed sesame seeds) is available in most supermarkets.

Chilling time	2 hours	2 hours
Serves	8	16
Calories per serving	170 (43 from fat)	170 (43 from fat)
Fat per serving	4.75 grams	4.75 grams

Perfect for those who are lactose intolerant, this creamy cheesecake has a nutty, mildly sweet taste.

1. Gently pat the prepared crust mixture on the bottom and sides of an 8-inch pie plate (or plates).

2. Blend together the tofu, tahini, chick peas, and sugar in a food processor. Add the soy milk, lemon juice, and vanilla. Continue to blend until smooth and well-combined.

3. Drizzle the gelatin over the mixture and fold in gently.

4. Pour the batter into the prepared crust (or crusts) and smooth with a spatula. Cover with plastic wrap and refrigerate at least 2 hours.

5. Cut into wedges and serve.

No-Bake
Chocolate Chip Cheesecake

INGREDIENT	ONE 8-INCH CAKE	TWO 8-INCH CAKES
Fat-free cream cheese, softened	2 8-ounce packages	4 8-ounce packages
Sugar	¾ cup	1½ cups
Low-fat whipped topping	½ cup	1 cup
Fat-free yogurt	¼ cup	½ cup
Fat-free sour cream	¼ cup	½ cup
Vanilla extract	1 teaspoon	2 teaspoons
Fresh lemon juice	½ teaspoon	1 teaspoon
Unflavored gelatin	1 tablespoon mixed with 1 tablespoon water	2 tablespoons mixed with 2 tablespoons water
Mini chocolate chips	½ cup	1 cup

CRUST

Graham Cracker (page 8)	single recipe	double recipe

Chilling time	2 hours	2 hours
Serves	8	16
Calories per serving	188 (18 from fat)	188 (18 from fat)
Fat per serving	2 grams	2 grams

This cheesecake has chocolaty appeal with a minimum of fat.

---

1. Gently pat the prepared crust mixture on the bottom and sides of an 8-inch pie plate (or plates).

2. Blend together the cream cheese and sugar with an electric mixer. Add the whipped topping, yogurt, sour cream, vanilla, and lemon juice. Continue to blend until smooth and well-combined.

3. Drizzle the gelatin over the mixture and fold in gently. Fold in the chocolate chips.

4. Pour the batter into the prepared crust (or crusts) and smooth with a spatula. Cover with plastic wrap and refrigerate at least 2 hours.

5. Cut into wedges and serve.

No-Bake Marble Swirl Cheesecake

INGREDIENT	ONE 8-INCH CAKE	TWO 8-INCH CAKES
Fat-free cream cheese, softened	2 8-ounce packages	4 8-ounce packages
Sugar	¾ cup	1½ cups
Low-fat whipped topping	½ cup	1 cup
Fat-free yogurt	¼ cup	½ cup
Fat-free sour cream	¼ cup	½ cup
Vanilla extract	1 teaspoon	2 teaspoons
Fresh lemon juice	½ teaspoon	1 teaspoon
European-style cocoa	⅓ cup	⅔ cup
Unflavored gelatin	1 tablespoon mixed with 1 tablespoon water	2 tablespoons mixed with 2 tablespoons water

CRUST

Graham Cracker (page 8)	single recipe	double recipe

Chilling time	2 hours	2 hours
Serves	8	16
Calories per serving	188 (18 from fat)	188 (18 from fat)
Fat per serving	2 grams	2 grams

Chocolate and vanilla are swirled together in this heavenly cheesecake.

---

1. Gently pat the prepared crust mixture on the bottom and sides of an 8-inch pie plate (or plates).

2. Blend together the cream cheese and sugar with an electric mixer. Add the whipped topping, yogurt, sour cream, vanilla, and lemon juice. Continue to blend until smooth and well-combined.

3. Drizzle the gelatin over the mixture and fold in gently.

4. Pour two-thirds of the batter into the prepared crust and smooth with a rubber spatula. Fold the cocoa into the remaining batter and drop it onto the vanilla batter. Quickly run a spatula through the chocolate to form a marble pattern.

5. Cover with plastic wrap and refrigerate at least 2 hours.

6. Cut into wedges and serve.

No-Bake Cheesecake Classics

No-Bake Chocolate Cheesecake

INGREDIENT	ONE 8-INCH CAKE	TWO 8-INCH CAKES
Fat-free cream cheese, softened	2 8-ounce packages	4 8-ounce packages
Sugar	¾ cup	1½ cups
Low-fat whipped topping	½ cup	1 cup
Fat-free yogurt	¼ cup	½ cup
Fat-free sour cream	¼ cup	½ cup
European-style cocoa	½ cup	1 cup
Vanilla extract	1 teaspoon	2 teaspoons
Fresh lemon juice	½ teaspoon	1 teaspoon
Unflavored gelatin	1 tablespoon mixed with 1 tablespoon water	2 tablespoons mixed with 2 tablespoons water

CRUST

Chocolate Graham Cracker (page 10)	single recipe	double recipe

Chilling time	2 hours	2 hours
Serves	8	16
Calories per serving	186 (18 from fat)	186 (18 from fat)
Fat per serving	2 grams	2 grams

Enjoy this creamy cheesecake with a mug of steaming hot chocolate.

---

1. Gently pat the prepared crust mixture on the bottom and sides of an 8-inch pie plate (or plates).

2. Blend together the cream cheese and sugar with an electric mixer. Add the whipped topping, yogurt, sour cream, cocoa, vanilla, and lemon juice. Continue to blend until smooth and well-combined.

3. Drizzle the gelatin over the mixture and fold in gently.

4. Pour the batter into the prepared crust (or crusts) and smooth with a spatula. Cover with plastic wrap and refrigerate at least 2 hours.

5. Cut into wedges and serve.

No-Bake
Mocha Cheesecake

INGREDIENT	ONE 8-INCH CAKE	TWO 8-INCH CAKES
Fat-free cream cheese, softened	2 8-ounce packages	4 8-ounce packages
Sugar	¾ cup	1½ cups
Low-fat whipped topping	½ cup	1 cup
Fat-free yogurt	¼ cup	½ cup
Fat-free sour cream	¼ cup	½ cup
European-style cocoa	½ cup	1 cup
Instant coffee granules	2 teaspoons	4 teaspoons
Vanilla extract	1 teaspoon	2 teaspoons
Fresh lemon juice	½ teaspoon	1 teaspoon
Unflavored gelatin	1 tablespoon mixed with 1 tablespoon water	2 tablespoons mixed with 2 tablespoons water

CRUST

Chocolate Graham Cracker (page 10)	single recipe	double recipe

Chilling time	2 hours	2 hours
Serves	8	16
Calories per serving	186 (18 from fat)	186 (18 from fat)
Fat per serving	2 grams	2 grams

Coffee and cocoa are united in this sensational treat.

---

1. Gently pat the prepared crust mixture on the bottom and sides of an 8-inch pie plate (or plates).

2. Blend together the cream cheese and sugar with an electric mixer. Add the whipped topping, yogurt, sour cream, cocoa, coffee granules, vanilla, and lemon juice. Continue to blend until smooth and well-combined.

3. Drizzle the gelatin over the mixture and fold in gently.

4. Pour the batter into the prepared crust (or crusts) and smooth with a spatula. Cover with plastic wrap and refrigerate at least 2 hours.

5. Cut into wedges and serve.

No-Bake Double Chocolate Cheesecake

INGREDIENT	ONE 8-INCH CAKE	TWO 8-INCH CAKES
Fat-free cream cheese, softened	2 8-ounce packages	4 8-ounce packages
Sugar	¾ cup	1½ cups
Low-fat whipped topping	½ cup	1 cup
Fat-free yogurt	¼ cup	½ cup
Fat-free sour cream	¼ cup	½ cup
European-style cocoa	½ cup	1 cup
Vanilla extract	1 teaspoon	2 teaspoons
Fresh lemon juice	½ teaspoon	1 teaspoon
Unflavored gelatin	1 tablespoon mixed with 1 tablespoon water	2 tablespoons mixed with 2 tablespoons water
Mini chocolate chips	¼ cup	½ cup

CRUST

Chocolate Graham Cracker (page 10)	single recipe	double recipe

Chilling time	2 hours	2 hours
Serves	8	16
Calories per serving	186 (23 from fat)	186 (23 from fat)
Fat per serving	2.6 grams	2.6 grams

For chocolate addicts only!

1. Gently pat the prepared crust mixture on the bottom and sides of an 8-inch pie plate (or plates).

2. Blend together the cream cheese and sugar with an electric mixer. Add the whipped topping, yogurt, sour cream, cocoa, vanilla, and lemon juice. Continue to blend until smooth and well-combined.

3. Drizzle the gelatin over the mixture and fold in gently. Fold in the chocolate chips.

4. Pour the batter into the prepared crust (or crusts) and smooth with a spatula. Cover with plastic wrap and refrigerate at least 2 hours.

5. Cut into wedges and serve.

No-Bake White Chocolate Cheesecake

INGREDIENT	ONE 8-INCH CAKE	TWO 8-INCH CAKES
Fat-free cream cheese, softened	2 8-ounce packages	4 8-ounce packages
Sugar	¾ cup	1½ cups
Low-fat whipped topping	½ cup	1 cup
Fat-free yogurt	¼ cup	½ cup
Fat-free sour cream	¼ cup	½ cup
White chocolate chips, melted	½ cup	1 cup
Vanilla extract	1 teaspoon	2 teaspoons
Fresh lemon juice	½ teaspoon	1 teaspoon
Unflavored gelatin	1 tablespoon mixed with 1 tablespoon water	2 tablespoons mixed with 2 tablespoons water

CRUST

Graham Cracker (page 8)	single recipe	double recipe

Chilling time	2 hours	2 hours
Serves	8	16
Calories per serving	211 (27 from fat)	211 (27 from fat)
Fat per serving	3 grams	3 grams

Heavenly white chocolate cheesecake is a snap with this recipe.

---

1. Gently pat the prepared crust mixture on the bottom and sides of an 8-inch pie plate (or plates).

2. Blend together the cream cheese and sugar with an electric mixer. Add the whipped topping, yogurt, sour cream, white chocolate, vanilla, and lemon juice. Continue to blend until smooth and well-combined.

3. Drizzle the gelatin over the mixture and fold in gently.

4. Pour the batter into the prepared crust (or crusts) and smooth with a spatula. Cover with plastic wrap and refrigerate at least 2 hours.

5. Cut into wedges and serve.

No-Bake Black-and-White Cheesecake

INGREDIENT	ONE 8-INCH CAKE	TWO 8-INCH CAKES
Fat-free cream cheese, softened	2 8-ounce packages	4 8-ounce packages
Sugar	¾ cup	1½ cups
Low-fat whipped topping	½ cup	1 cup
Fat-free yogurt	¼ cup	½ cup
Fat-free sour cream	¼ cup	½ cup
European-style cocoa	½ cup	1 cup
Vanilla extract	1 teaspoon	2 teaspoons
Fresh lemon juice	½ teaspoon	1 teaspoon
Unflavored gelatin	1 tablespoon mixed with 1 tablespoon water	2 tablespoons mixed with 2 tablespoons water
White chocolate chips	¼ cup	½ cup
CRUST		
Chocolate Graham Cracker (page 10)	single recipe	double recipe

Chilling time	2 hours	2 hours
Serves	8	16
Calories per serving	224 (32 from fat)	224 (32 from fat)
Fat per serving	3.6 grams	3.6 grams

Rich, creamy chocolate flecked with sweet white chocolate chips makes for a very special cheesecake.

---

1. Gently pat the prepared crust mixture on the bottom and sides of an 8-inch pie plate (or plates).

2. Blend together the cream cheese and sugar with an electric mixer. Add the whipped topping, yogurt, sour cream, cocoa, vanilla, and lemon juice. Continue to blend until smooth and well-combined.

3. Drizzle the gelatin over the mixture and fold in gently. Fold in the chocolate chips.

4. Pour the batter into the prepared crust (or crusts) and smooth with a spatula. Cover with plastic wrap and refrigerate at least 2 hours.

5. Cut into wedges and serve.

No-Bake
Milk Chocolate Cheesecake

INGREDIENT	ONE 8-INCH CAKE	TWO 8-INCH CAKES
Fat-free cream cheese, softened	2 8-ounce packages	4 8-ounce packages
Sugar	¾ cup	1½ cups
Low-fat whipped topping	½ cup	1 cup
Fat-free yogurt	¼ cup	½ cup
Fat-free sour cream	¼ cup	½ cup
Milk chocolate chips, melted	½ cup	1 cup
Vanilla extract	1 teaspoon	2 teaspoons
Fresh lemon juice	½ teaspoon	1 teaspoon
Unflavored gelatin	1 tablespoon mixed with 1 tablespoon water	2 tablespoons mixed with 2 tablespoons water

CRUST

Chocolate Graham Cracker (page 10)	single recipe	double recipe

Chilling time	2 hours	2 hours
Serves	8	16
Calories per serving	211 (27 from fat)	211 (27 from fat)
Fat per serving	3 grams	3 grams

Rich, creamy, and chocolaty good.

1. Gently pat the prepared crust mixture on the bottom and sides of an 8-inch pie plate (or plates).

2. Blend together the cream cheese and sugar with an electric mixer. Add the whipped topping, yogurt, sour cream, chocolate, vanilla, and lemon juice. Continue to blend until smooth and well-combined.

3. Drizzle the gelatin over the mixture and fold in gently.

4. Pour the batter into the prepared crust (or crusts) and smooth with a spatula. Cover with plastic wrap and refrigerate at least 2 hours.

5. Cut into wedges and serve.

No-Bake
Melon Cheesecake

INGREDIENT	ONE 8-INCH CAKE	TWO 8-INCH CAKES
Fat-free cream cheese, softened	2 8-ounce packages	4 8-ounce packages
Sugar	¾ cup	1½ cups
Low-fat whipped topping	½ cup	1 cup
Fat-free yogurt	¼ cup	½ cup
Fat-free sour cream	¼ cup	½ cup
Vanilla extract	1 teaspoon	2 teaspoons
Fresh lemon juice	½ teaspoon	1 teaspoon
Unflavored gelatin	1 tablespoon mixed with 1 tablespoon water	2 tablespoons mixed with 2 tablespoons water
Puréed honeydew melon, well-drained	½ cup	1 cup
CRUST		
Chewy Oat (page 22)	single recipe	double recipe

Chilling time	2 hours	2 hours
Serves	8	16
Calories per serving	149 (9 from fat)	149 (9 from fat)
Fat per serving	1 gram	1 gram

Delicate and sweet—the perfect summer treat.

---

1. Gently pat the prepared crust mixture on the bottom and sides of an 8-inch pie plate (or plates).

2. Blend together the cream cheese and sugar with an electric mixer. Add the whipped topping, yogurt, sour cream, vanilla, and lemon juice. Continue to blend until smooth and well-combined.

3. Drizzle the gelatin over the mixture and fold in gently. Fold in the melon.

4. Pour the batter into the prepared crust (or crusts) and smooth with a spatula. Cover with plastic wrap and refrigerate at least 2 hours.

5. Cut into wedges and serve.

Variations

For other luscious versions of this cheesecake, use puréed peaches or mangoes.

No-Bake Mandarin Orange Cheesecake

INGREDIENT	ONE 8-INCH CAKE	TWO 8-INCH CAKES
Fat-free cream cheese, softened	2 8-ounce packages	4 8-ounce packages
Sugar	¾ cup	1½ cups
Low-fat whipped topping	½ cup	1 cup
Fat-free yogurt	¼ cup	½ cup
Fat-free sour cream	¼ cup	½ cup
Orange extract	1 teaspoon	2 teaspoons
Vanilla extract	1 teaspoon	2 teaspoons
Fresh lemon juice	½ teaspoon	1 teaspoon
Orange food coloring	2 drops	4 drops
Unflavored gelatin	1 tablespoon mixed with 1 tablespoon water	2 tablespoons mixed with 2 tablespoons water
Mandarin oranges, drained and chopped	½ cup	1 cup
CRUST		
Zesty Orange Oat (page 24)	single recipe	double recipe

Chilling time	2 hours	2 hours
Serves	8	16
Calories per serving	149 (9 from fat)	149 (9 from fat)
Fat per serving	1 gram	1 gram

The Zesty Orange Graham Cracker Crust (page 12) is another perfect foundation for this cheesecake.

---

1. Gently pat the prepared crust mixture on the bottom and sides of an 8-inch pie plate (or plates).

2. Blend together the cream cheese and sugar with an electric mixer. Add the whipped topping, yogurt, sour cream, orange and vanilla extracts, lemon juice, and food coloring. Continue to blend until smooth and well-combined.

3. Drizzle the gelatin over the mixture and fold in gently. Fold in the mandarin oranges.

4. Pour the batter into the prepared crust (or crusts) and smooth with a spatula. Cover with plastic wrap and refrigerate at least 2 hours.

5. Cut into wedges and serve.

No-Bake Strawberry Cheesecake

INGREDIENT	ONE 8-INCH CAKE	TWO 8-INCH CAKES
Fat-free cream cheese, softened	1 8-ounce package	2 8-ounce packages
Tofu, mashed	8 ounces	16 ounces
Sugar	¾ cup	1½ cups
Low-fat whipped topping	½ cup	1 cup
Fat-free yogurt	¼ cup	½ cup
Fat-free sour cream	¼ cup	½ cup
All-fruit strawberry jam	¼ cup	½ cup
Vanilla extract	1 teaspoon	2 teaspoons
Fresh lemon juice	½ teaspoon	1 teaspoon
Unflavored gelatin	1 tablespoon mixed with 1 tablespoon water	2 tablespoons mixed with 2 tablespoons water
Sliced strawberries, fresh or frozen*	½ cup	1 cup

CRUST

Chewy Oat (page 22)	single recipe	double recipe

* Be sure to thaw and drain if using frozen variety.

Chilling time	2 hours	2 hours
Serves	8	16
Calories per serving	194 (25 from fat)	194 (25 from fat)
Fat per serving	2.75 grams	2.75 grams

Sweet strawberries stand center stage in this tofu-based no-bake dessert.

---

1. Gently pat the prepared crust mixture on the bottom and sides of an 8-inch pie plate (or plates).

2. Blend together the cream cheese, tofu, and sugar with an electric mixer. Add the whipped topping, yogurt, sour cream, jam, vanilla, and lemon juice. Continue to blend until smooth and well-combined.

3. Drizzle the gelatin over the mixture and fold in gently. Fold in the strawberries.

4. Pour the batter into the prepared crust (or crusts) and smooth with a spatula. Cover with plastic wrap and refrigerate at least 2 hours.

5. Cut into wedges and serve.

No-Bake Cherry Cheesecake

INGREDIENT	ONE 8-INCH CAKE	TWO 8-INCH CAKES
Fat-free cream cheese, softened	1 8-ounce package	2 8-ounce packages
Tofu, mashed	8 ounces	16 ounces
Sugar	¾ cup	1½ cups
Low-fat whipped topping	½ cup	1 cup
Fat-free yogurt	¼ cup	½ cup
Fat-free sour cream	¼ cup	½ cup
Cherry extract	1 teaspoon	2 teaspoons
Vanilla extract	1 teaspoon	2 teaspoons
Fresh lemon juice	½ teaspoon	1 teaspoon
Red food coloring (optional)	2 drops	4 drops
Unflavored gelatin	1 tablespoon mixed with 1 tablespoon water	2 tablespoons mixed with 2 tablespoons water
Dark sweet cherries, chopped	½ cup	1 cup
CRUST		
Chewy Oat (page 22)	single recipe	double recipe

Chilling time	2 hours	2 hours
Serves	8	16
Calories per serving	195 (25 from fat)	195 (25 from fat)
Fat per serving	2.75 grams	2.75 grams

This cheesecake, with its sweet, juicy cherries, always gets rave reviews.

1. Gently pat the prepared crust mixture on the bottom and sides of an 8-inch pie plate (or plates).

2. Blend together the cream cheese, tofu, and sugar with an electric mixer. Add the whipped topping, yogurt, sour cream, cherry and vanilla extracts, lemon juice, and food coloring. Continue to blend until smooth and well-combined.

3. Drizzle the gelatin over the mixture and fold in gently. Fold in the cherries.

4. Pour the batter into the prepared crust (or crusts) and smooth with a spatula. Cover with plastic wrap and refrigerate at least 2 hours.

5. Cut into wedges and serve.

No-Bake Raspberry Cheesecake

INGREDIENT	ONE 8-INCH CAKE	TWO 8-INCH CAKES
Fat-free cream cheese, softened	1 8-ounce package	2 8-ounce packages
Tofu, mashed	8 ounces	16 ounces
Sugar	¾ cup	1½ cups
Low-fat whipped topping	½ cup	1 cup
Fat-free yogurt	¼ cup	½ cup
Fat-free sour cream	¼ cup	½ cup
Vanilla extract	1 teaspoon	2 teaspoons
Fresh lemon juice	½ teaspoon	1 teaspoon
Unflavored gelatin	1 tablespoon mixed with 1 tablespoon water	2 tablespoons mixed with 2 tablespoons water
Puréed raspberries, fresh or frozen*	½ cup	1 cup

CRUST

Graham Cracker (page 8)	single recipe	double recipe

* Be sure to thaw and drain if using frozen variety.

Chilling time	2 hours	2 hours
Serves	8	16
Calories per serving	195 (25 from fat)	195 (25 from fat)
Fat per serving	2.75 grams	2.75 grams

Fresh raspberries make this cheesecake extra special.

---

1. Gently pat the prepared crust mixture on the bottom and sides of an 8-inch pie plate (or plates).

2. Blend together the cream cheese, tofu, and sugar with an electric mixer. Add the whipped topping, yogurt, sour cream, vanilla, and lemon juice. Continue to blend until smooth and well-combined.

3. Drizzle the gelatin over the mixture and fold in gently. Fold in the raspberries.

4. Pour the batter into the prepared crust (or crusts) and smooth with a spatula. Cover with plastic wrap and refrigerate at least 2 hours.

5. Cut into wedges and serve.

Variations

Instead of raspberries, use blackberries or a mixture of your favorite berries.

No-Bake Lime Cheesecake

INGREDIENT	ONE 8-INCH CAKE	TWO 8-INCH CAKES
Fat-free cream cheese, softened	2 8-ounce packages	4 8-ounce packages
Sugar	¾ cup	1½ cups
Low-fat whipped topping	½ cup	1 cup
Fat-free yogurt	¼ cup	½ cup
Fat-free sour cream	¼ cup	½ cup
Lime juice	¼ cup	½ cup
Vanilla extract	1 teaspoon	2 teaspoons
Green food coloring	2 drops	4 drops
Unflavored gelatin	1 tablespoon mixed with 1 tablespoon water	2 tablespoons mixed with 2 tablespoons water
CRUST		
Zesty Lime Oat (page 28)	single recipe	double recipe

Chilling Time	2 hours	2 hours
Serves	8	16
Calories per serving	171 (9 from fat)	171 (9 from fat)
Fat per serving	1 gram	1 gram

Whip up this cool, light cheesecake in a flash.

---

1. Gently pat the prepared crust mixture on the bottom and sides of an 8-inch pie plate (or plates).

2. Blend together the cream cheese and sugar with an electric mixer. Add the whipped topping, yogurt, sour cream, lime juice, vanilla, and food coloring. Continue to blend until smooth and well-combined.

3. Drizzle the gelatin over the mixture and fold in gently.

4. Pour the batter into the prepared crust (or crusts) and smooth with a spatula. Cover with plastic wrap and refrigerate at least 2 hours.

5. Cut into wedges and serve.

No-Bake Lemon Cheesecake

INGREDIENT	ONE 8-INCH CAKE	TWO 8-INCH CAKES
Fat-free cream cheese, softened	2 8-ounce packages	4 8-ounce packages
Sugar	¾ cup	1½ cups
Low-fat whipped topping	½ cup	1 cup
Fat-free yogurt	¼ cup	½ cup
Fat-free sour cream	¼ cup	½ cup
Fresh lemon juice	⅓ cup	⅔ cup
Vanilla extract	1 teaspoon	2 teaspoons
Unflavored gelatin	1 tablespoon mixed with 1 tablespoon water	2 tablespoons mixed with 2 tablespoons water

CRUST

Lemony Graham Cracker (page 14)	single recipe	double recipe

Chilling time	2 hours	2 hours
Serves	8	16
Calories per serving	171 (9 from fat)	171 (9 from fat)
Fat per serving	1 gram	1 gram

A light and luscious lemon-lover's delight.

---

1. Gently pat the prepared crust mixture on the bottom and sides of an 8-inch pie plate (or plates).

2. Blend together the cream cheese and sugar with an electric mixer. Add the whipped topping, yogurt, sour cream, lemon juice, vanilla, and food coloring. Continue to blend until smooth and well-combined.

3. Drizzle the gelatin over the mixture and fold in gently.

4. Pour the batter into the prepared crust (or crusts) and smooth with a spatula. Cover with plastic wrap and refrigerate at least 2 hours.

5. Cut into wedges and serve.

No-Bake
Piña Colada

INGREDIENT	ONE 8-INCH CAKE	TWO 8-INCH CAKES
Fat-free cream cheese, softened	2 8-ounce packages	4 8-ounce packages
Sugar	¾ cup	1½ cups
Low-fat whipped topping	½ cup	1 cup
Fat-free yogurt	¼ cup	½ cup
Fat-free sour cream	¼ cup	½ cup
Coconut extract	1 teaspoon	2 teaspoons
Vanilla extract	1 teaspoon	2 teaspoons
Fresh lemon juice	½ teaspoon	1 teaspoon
Unflavored gelatin	1 tablespoon mixed with 1 tablespoon water	2 tablespoons mixed with 2 tablespoons water
Crushed pineapple, drained	½ cup	1 cup
CRUST		
Coconut Graham Cracker (page 20)	single recipe	double recipe

Chilling time	2 hours	2 hours
Serves	8	16
Calories per serving	148 (9 from fat)	148 (9 from fat)
Fat per serving	1 gram	1 gram

A cool and creamy taste of the tropics.

---

1. Gently pat the prepared crust mixture on the bottom and sides of an 8-inch pie plate (or plates).

2. Blend together the cream cheese and sugar with an electric mixer. Add the whipped topping, yogurt, sour cream, coconut and vanilla extracts, and lemon juice. Continue to blend until smooth and well-combined.

3. Drizzle the gelatin over the mixture and fold in gently. Fold in the pineapple.

4. Pour the batter into the prepared crust (or crusts) and smooth with a spatula. Cover with plastic wrap and refrigerate at least 2 hours.

5. Cut into wedges and serve.

No-Bake
Banana Colada

INGREDIENT	ONE 8-INCH CAKE	TWO 8-INCH CAKES
Fat-free cream cheese, softened	2 8-ounce packages	4 8-ounce packages
Sugar	¾ cup	1½ cups
Low-fat whipped topping	½ cup	1 cup
Fat-free yogurt	¼ cup	½ cup
Fat-free sour cream	¼ cup	½ cup
Banana extract	1 teaspoon	2 teaspoons
Vanilla extract	1 teaspoon	2 teaspoons
Fresh lemon juice	½ teaspoon	1 teaspoon
Unflavored gelatin	1 tablespoon mixed with 1 tablespoon water	2 tablespoons mixed with 2 tablespoons water
Puréed bananas	½ cup	1 cup

CRUST

Graham Cracker (page 8)	single recipe	double recipe

Chilling time	2 hours	2 hours
Serves	8	16
Calories per serving	150 (9 from fat)	150 (9 from fat)
Fat per serving	1 gram	1 gram

One taste of this tropical cheesecake will transport you to an island paradise.

1. Gently pat the prepared crust mixture on the bottom and sides of an 8-inch pie plate (or plates).

2. Blend together the cream cheese and sugar with an electric mixer. Add the whipped topping, yogurt, sour cream, banana and vanilla extracts, and lemon juice. Continue to blend until smooth and well-combined.

3. Drizzle the gelatin over the mixture and fold in gently. Fold in the puréed bananas.

4. Pour the batter into the prepared crust (or crusts) and smooth with a spatula. Cover with plastic wrap and refrigerate at least 2 hours.

5. Cut into wedges and serve.

No-Bake Peppermint Cheesecake

INGREDIENT	ONE 8-INCH CAKE	TWO 8-INCH CAKES
Fat-free cream cheese, softened	2 8-ounce packages	4 8-ounce packages
Sugar	¾ cup	1½ cups
Low-fat whipped topping	½ cup	1 cup
Fat-free yogurt	¼ cup	½ cup
Fat-free sour cream	¼ cup	½ cup
Peppermint extract	1 teaspoon	2 teaspoons
Vanilla extract	1 teaspoon	2 teaspoons
Fresh lemon juice	½ teaspoon	1 teaspoon
Unflavored gelatin	1 tablespoon mixed with 1 tablespoon water	2 tablespoons mixed with 2 tablespoons water
Peppermint candy, crushed	½ cup	1 cup
CRUST		
Graham Cracker (page 8)	single recipe	double recipe

Chilling time	2 hours	2 hours
Serves	8	16
Calories per serving	204 (9 from fat)	204 (9 from fat)
Fat per serving	1 gram	1 gram

There are no cheesecakes "cooler" than this one.

1. Gently pat the prepared crust mixture on the bottom and sides of an 8-inch pie plate (or plates).

2. Blend together the cream cheese and sugar with an electric mixer. Add the whipped topping, yogurt, sour cream, peppermint and vanilla extracts, and lemon juice. Continue to blend until smooth and well-combined.

3. Drizzle the gelatin over the mixture and fold in gently. Fold in the peppermint candy.

4. Pour the batter into the prepared crust (or crusts) and smooth with a spatula. Cover with plastic wrap and refrigerate at least 2 hours.

5. Cut into wedges and serve.

Variation

For another "cool" version of this cake, use spearmint extract and candies instead of peppermint.

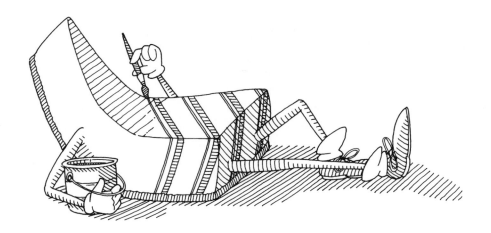

No-Bake
Cinnamon Cheesecake

INGREDIENT	ONE 8-INCH CAKE	TWO 8-INCH CAKES
Fat-free cream cheese, softened	2 8-ounce packages	4 8-ounce packages
Sugar	¾ cup	1½ cups
Low-fat whipped topping	½ cup	1 cup
Fat-free yogurt	¼ cup	½ cup
Fat-free sour cream	¼ cup	½ cup
Ground cinnamon	2 teaspoons	4 teaspoons
Vanilla extract	1 teaspoon	2 teaspoons
Fresh lemon juice	½ teaspoon	1 teaspoon
Unflavored gelatin	1 tablespoon mixed with 1 tablespoon water	2 tablespoons mixed with 2 tablespoons water
Mini cinnamon jelly beans	½ cup	1 cup
CRUST		
Graham Cracker (page 8)	single recipe	double recipe

Chilling time	2 hours	2 hours
Serves	8	16
Calories per serving	208 (9 from fat)	208 (9 from fat)
Fat per serving	1 gram	1 gram

Ground cinnamon and cinnamon-flavored jelly beans give this cheesecake its unique flavor.

---

1. Gently pat the prepared crust mixture on the bottom and sides of an 8-inch pie plate (or plates).

2. Blend together the cream cheese and sugar with an electric mixer. Add the whipped topping, yogurt, sour cream, cinnamon, vanilla, and lemon juice. Continue to blend until smooth and well-combined.

3. Drizzle the gelatin over the mixture and fold in gently. Fold in the jelly beans.

4. Pour the batter into the prepared crust (or crusts) and smooth with a spatula. Cover with plastic wrap and refrigerate at least 2 hours.

5. Cut into wedges and serve.

No-Bake
Ginger Snap Cheesecake

INGREDIENT	ONE 8-INCH CAKE	TWO 8-INCH CAKES
Fat-free cream cheese, softened	2 8-ounce packages	4 8-ounce packages
Sugar	¾ cup	1½ cups
Low-fat whipped topping	½ cup	1 cup
Fat-free yogurt	¼ cup	½ cup
Fat-free sour cream	¼ cup	½ cup
Ground ginger	2 teaspoons	4 teaspoons
Vanilla extract	1 teaspoon	2 teaspoons
Fresh lemon juice	½ teaspoon	1 teaspoon
Unflavored gelatin	1 tablespoon mixed with 1 tablespoon water	2 tablespoons mixed with 2 tablespoons water
Gingersnap cookies, crushed	½ cup	1 cup

CRUST

Graham Cracker (page 8)	single recipe	double recipe

Chilling time	2 hours	2 hours
Serves	8	16
Calories per serving	184 (9 from fat)	184 (9 from fat)
Fat per serving	1 gram	1 gram

This is a popular choice with the kids.

1. Gently pat the prepared crust mixture on the bottom and sides of an 8-inch pie plate (or plates).

2. Blend together the cream cheese and sugar with an electric mixer. Add the whipped topping, yogurt, sour cream, ginger, vanilla, and lemon juice. Continue to blend until smooth and well-combined.

3. Drizzle the gelatin over the mixture and fold in gently. Fold in the gingersnaps.

4. Pour the batter into the prepared crust (or crusts) and smooth with a spatula. Cover with plastic wrap and refrigerate at least 2 hours.

5. Cut into wedges and serve.

No-Bake Peanut Butter and Chocolate Cheesecake

INGREDIENT	ONE 8-INCH CAKE	TWO 8-INCH CAKES
Fat-free cream cheese, softened	2 8-ounce packages	4 8-ounce packages
Sugar	¾ cup	1½ cups
Low-fat whipped topping	½ cup	½ cup
Fat-free yogurt	¼ cup	½ cup
Fat-free sour cream	¼ cup	½ cup
Reduced-fat peanut butter	¼ cup	½ cup
Vanilla extract	1 teaspoon	2 teaspoons
Fresh lemon juice	½ teaspoon	1 teaspoon
Unflavored gelatin	1 tablespoon mixed with 1 tablespoon water	2 tablespoons mixed with 2 tablespoons water
Mini chocolate chips	¼ cup	½ cup
CRUST		
Graham Cracker (page 8)	single recipe	double recipe

Chilling time	2 hours	2 hours
Serves	8	16
Calories per serving	236 (45 from fat)	236 (45 from fat)
Fat per serving	5 grams	5 grams

When you feel the need to splurge, this creamy peanut butter and rich chocolate cheesecake will fit the bill.

---

1. Gently pat the prepared crust mixture on the bottom and sides of an 8-inch pie plate (or plates).

2. Blend together the cream cheese and sugar with an electric mixer. Add the whipped topping, yogurt, sour cream, peanut butter, vanilla, and lemon juice. Continue to blend until smooth and well-combined.

3. Drizzle the gelatin over the mixture and fold in gently. Fold in the chocolate chips.

4. Pour the batter into the prepared crust (or crusts) and smooth with a spatula. Cover with plastic wrap and refrigerate at least 2 hours.

5. Cut into wedges and serve.

No-Bake Creamy Root Beer Cheesecake

INGREDIENT	ONE 8-INCH CAKE	TWO 8-INCH CAKES
Fat-free cream cheese, softened	2 8-ounce packages	4 8-ounce packages
Sugar	¾ cup	1½ cups
Low-fat whipped topping	½ cup	1 cup
Fat-free yogurt	¼ cup	½ cup
Fat-free sour cream	¼ cup	½ cup
Root beer extract	1 teaspoon	2 teaspoons
Vanilla extract	1 teaspoon	2 teaspoons
Fresh lemon juice	½ teaspoon	1 teaspoon
Unflavored gelatin	1 tablespoon mixed with 1 tablespoon water	2 tablespoons mixed with 2 tablespoons water
Mini root beer jelly beans	½ cup	1 cup
CRUST		
Graham Cracker (page 8)	single recipe	double recipe

Chilling time	2 hours	2 hours
Serves	8	16
Calories per serving	208 (9 from fat)	208 (9 from fat)
Fat per serving	1 gram	1 gram

This creamy unusual-flavored cheesecake is a real taste treat.

1. Gently pat the prepared crust mixture on the bottom and sides of an 8-inch pie plate (or plates).

2. Blend together the cream cheese and sugar with an electric mixer. Add the whipped topping, yogurt, sour cream, root beer and vanilla extracts, and lemon juice. Continue to blend until smooth and well-combined.

3. Drizzle the gelatin over the mixture and fold in gently. Fold in the jelly beans.

4. Pour the batter into the prepared crust (or crusts) and smooth with a spatula. Cover with plastic wrap and refrigerate at least 2 hours.

5. Cut into wedges and serve.

No-Bake Caramel Cheesecake

INGREDIENT	ONE 8-INCH CAKE	TWO 8-INCH CAKES
Fat-free cream cheese, softened	2 8-ounce packages	4 8-ounce packages
Sugar	¾ cup	1½ cups
Low-fat whipped topping	½ cup	1 cup
Fat-free yogurt	¼ cup	½ cup
Fat-free sour cream	¼ cup	½ cup
Fat-free caramel ice cream topping	½ cup	1 cup
Vanilla extract	1 teaspoon	2 teaspoons
Fresh lemon juice	½ teaspoon	1 teaspoon
Unflavored gelatin	1 tablespoon mixed with 1 tablespoon water	2 tablespoons mixed with 2 tablespoons water

CRUST

Graham Cracker (page 8)	single recipe	double recipe

Chilling time	2 hours	2 hours
Serves	8	16
Calories per serving	226 (9 from fat)	226 (9 from fat)
Fat per serving	1 gram	1 gram

Tastes like a scrumptious ice cream sundae.

---

1. Gently pat the prepared crust mixture on the bottom and sides of an 8-inch pie plate (or plates).

2. Blend together the cream cheese and sugar with an electric mixer. Add the whipped topping, yogurt, sour cream, caramel topping, vanilla, and lemon juice. Continue to blend until smooth and well-combined.

3. Drizzle the gelatin over the mixture and fold in gently.

4. Pour the batter into the prepared crust (or crusts) and smooth with a spatula. Cover with plastic wrap and refrigerate at least 2 hours.

5. Cut into wedges and serve.

Variation

For a butterscotch treat, use fat-free butterscotch ice cream topping instead of caramel.

No-Bake Maple Cheesecake

INGREDIENT	ONE 8-INCH CAKE	TWO 8-INCH CAKES
Fat-free cream cheese, softened	2 8-ounce packages	4 8-ounce packages
Sugar	¾ cup	1½ cups
Low-fat whipped topping	½ cup	1 cup
Fat-free yogurt	¼ cup	½ cup
Fat-free sour cream	¼ cup	½ cup
Maple extract	1 teaspoon	2 teaspoons
Vanilla extract	1 teaspoon	2 teaspoons
Fresh lemon juice	½ teaspoon	1 teaspoon
Unflavored gelatin	1 tablespoon mixed with 1 tablespoon water	2 tablespoons mixed with 2 tablespoons water

CRUST

Graham Cracker (page 8)	single recipe	double recipe

Chilling time	2 hours	2 hours
Serves	8	16
Calories per serving	228 (11 from fat)	228 (11 from fat)
Fat per serving	1.3 grams	1.3 grams

You can substitute one third cup pure maple syrup for the maple extract in this recipe.

---

1. Gently pat the prepared crust mixture on the bottom and sides of an 8-inch pie plate (or plates).

2. Blend together the cream cheese and sugar with an electric mixer. Add the whipped topping, yogurt, sour cream, maple and vanilla extracts, and lemon juice. Continue to blend until smooth and well-combined.

3. Drizzle the gelatin over the mixture and fold in gently.

4. Pour the batter into the prepared crust (or crusts) and smooth with a spatula. Cover with plastic wrap and refrigerate at least 2 hours.

5. Cut into wedges and serve.

No-Bake
Rose Petal Cheesecake

INGREDIENT	ONE 8-INCH CAKE	TWO 8-INCH CAKES
Fat-free cream cheese, softened	2 8-ounce packages	4 8-ounce packages
Sugar	¾ cup	1½ cups
Low-fat whipped topping	½ cup	1 cup
Fat-free yogurt	¼ cup	½ cup
Fat-free sour cream	¼ cup	½ cup
Rose syrup*	⅓ cup	⅔ cup
Vanilla extract	1 teaspoon	2 teaspoons
Fresh lemon juice	½ teaspoon	1 teaspoon
Unflavored gelatin	1 tablespoon mixed with 1 tablespoon water	2 tablespoons mixed with 2 tablespoons water

CRUST

Graham Cracker (page 8)	single recipe	double recipe

* Rose syrup is available in Greek and Middle Eastern markets. To make your own, see the recipe on page 154.

Chilling time	2 hours	2 hours
Serves	8	16
Calories per serving	205 (9 from fat)	205 (9 from fat)
Fat per serving	1 gram	1 gram

This delicate rose-flavored cheesecake is the perfect dessert for that special dinner party.

---

1. Gently pat the prepared crust mixture on the bottom and sides of an 8-inch pie plate (or plates).

2. Blend together the cream cheese and sugar with an electric mixer. Add the whipped topping, yogurt, sour cream, rose syrup, vanilla, and lemon juice. Continue to blend until smooth and well-combined.

3. Drizzle the gelatin over the mixture and fold in gently.

4. Pour the batter into the prepared crust (or crusts) and smooth with a spatula. Cover with plastic wrap and refrigerate at least 2 hours.

5. Cut into wedges and serve.

10.

No-Bake
Layered Sensations

Colorful contrasting layers make the flavorful no-bake cheesecakes in this chapter as beautiful as they are delicious. And while these delectable layered cakes may look complicated to make, nothing could be further from the truth. They are both quick and easy to prepare. Most of the flavor combinations are the same as the ones found in Chapter 8, but, as usual, feel free to use your own favorite flavor selections.

No-Bake Triple
Treat Cheesecake

INGREDIENT	ONE 8-INCH CAKE	TWO 8-INCH CAKES
Fat-free cream cheese, softened	2 8-ounce packages	4 8-ounce packages
Sugar	¾ cup	1½ cups
Low-fat whipped topping	½ cup	1 cup
Fat-free yogurt	¼ cup	½ cup
Fat-free sour cream	¼ cup	½ cup
Vanilla extract	1 teaspoon	2 teaspoons
Fresh lemon juice	½ teaspoon	1 teaspoon
Unflavored gelatin	1 tablespoon mixed with 1 tablespoon water	2 tablespoons mixed with 2 tablespoons water
European-style cocoa	⅓ cup	⅔ cup
Puréed strawberries, fresh or frozen*	½ cup	1 cup

CRUST

Chocolate Graham Cracker (page 10)	single recipe	double recipe

* Be sure to thaw and drain if using frozen variety.

Chilling time	2 hours	2 hours
Serves	8	16
Calories per serving	183 (9 from fat)	183 (9 from fat)
Fat per serving	1 gram	1 gram

Luscious layers of vanilla, chocolate, and strawberry make up this creamy no-bake cake, but feel free to combine any three flavors for your personal triple treat.

---

1. Gently pat the prepared crust mixture on the bottom and sides of an 8-inch pie plate (or plates).

2. Blend together the cream cheese and sugar with an electric mixer. Add the whipped topping, yogurt, sour cream, vanilla, and lemon juice. Continue to blend until smooth and well-combined.

3. Drizzle the gelatin over the mixture and fold in gently.

4. Divide the batter into thirds. Fold the cocoa into one third, the strawberries into another, and leave the last one plain.

5. Pour the cocoa batter into the prepared crust (or crusts) and smooth with a spatula. Gently spoon the strawberry batter on top, then follow with the vanilla batter.

6. Cover with plastic wrap and refrigerate at least 2 hours.

7. Cut into wedges and serve.

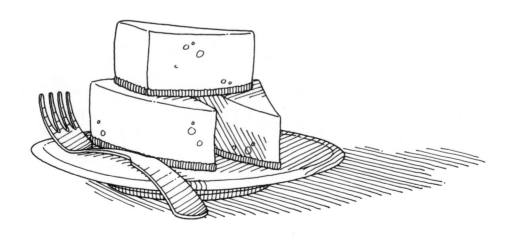

No-Bake Chocolate and Cream Cheesecake

INGREDIENT	ONE 8-INCH CAKE	TWO 8-INCH CAKES
Fat-free cream cheese, softened	2 8-ounce packages	4 8-ounce packages
Sugar	¾ cup	1½ cups
Low-fat whipped topping	½ cup	1 cup
Fat-free yogurt	¼ cup	½ cup
Fat-free sour cream	¼ cup	½ cup
Vanilla extract	1 teaspoon	2 teaspoons
Fresh lemon juice	½ teaspoon	1 teaspoon
Unflavored gelatin	1 tablespoon mixed with 1 tablespoon water	2 tablespoons mixed with 2 tablespoons water
European-style cocoa	⅓ cup	⅔ cup
CRUST		
Chocolate Graham Cracker (page 10)	single recipe	double recipe

Chilling time	2 hours	2 hours
Serves	8	16
Calories per serving	180 (14 from fat)	180 (14 from fat)
Fat per serving	1.6 grams	1.6 grams

The perfect choice for chocolate cream pie lovers.

---

1. Gently pat the prepared crust mixture on the bottom and sides of an 8-inch pie plate (or plates).

2. Blend together the cream cheese and sugar with an electric mixer. Add the whipped topping, yogurt, sour cream, vanilla, and lemon juice. Continue to blend until smooth and well-combined.

3. Drizzle the gelatin over the mixture and fold in gently.

4. Divide the batter in half. Fold the cocoa into one half, and leave the other half plain.

5. Pour the cocoa batter into the prepared crust (or crusts) and smooth with a spatula. Gently spoon the vanilla batter on top.

6. Cover with plastic wrap and refrigerate at least 2 hours.

7. Cut into wedges and serve.

No-Bake Chocolate Strawberry Cheesecake

INGREDIENT	ONE 8-INCH CAKE	TWO 8-INCH CAKES
Fat-free cream cheese, softened	2 8-ounce packages	4 8-ounce packages
Sugar	¾ cup	1½ cups
Low-fat whipped topping	½ cup	1 cup
Fat-free yogurt	¼ cup	½ cup
Fat-free sour cream	¼ cup	½ cup
Vanilla extract	1 teaspoon	2 teaspoons
Fresh lemon juice	½ teaspoon	1 teaspoon
Unflavored gelatin	1 tablespoon mixed with 1 tablespoon water	2 tablespoons mixed with 2 tablespoons water
European-style cocoa	⅓ cup	⅔ cup
Puréed strawberries, fresh or frozen*	½ cup	1 cup

CRUST		
Chocolate Graham Cracker (page 10)	single recipe	double recipe

* Be sure to thaw and drain if using frozen variety.

Chilling time	2 hours	2 hours
Serves	8	16
Calories per serving	183 (9 from fat)	183 (9 from fat)
Fat per serving	1 gram	1 gram

You can use fresh or frozen strawberries for this cake.

1. Gently pat the prepared crust mixture on the bottom and sides of an 8-inch pie plate (or plates).

2. Blend together the cream cheese and sugar with an electric mixer. Add the whipped topping, yogurt, sour cream, vanilla, and lemon juice. Continue to blend until smooth and well-combined.

3. Drizzle the gelatin over the mixture and fold in gently.

4. Divide the batter in half. Fold the cocoa into one half, and the strawberries into the other.

5. Pour the cocoa batter into the prepared crust (or crusts) and smooth with a spatula. Gently spoon the strawberry batter on top.

6. Cover with plastic wrap and refrigerate at least 2 hours.

7. Cut into wedges and serve.

No-Bake Chocolate Cherry Cheesecake

INGREDIENT	ONE 8-INCH CAKE	TWO 8-INCH CAKES
Fat-free cream cheese, softened	2 8-ounce packages	4 8-ounce packages
Sugar	¾ cup	1½ cups
Low-fat whipped topping	½ cup	1 cup
Fat-free yogurt	¼ cup	½ cup
Fat-free sour cream	¼ cup	½ cup
Vanilla extract	1 teaspoon	2 teaspoons
Fresh lemon juice	½ teaspoon	1 teaspoon
Unflavored gelatin	1 tablespoon mixed with 1 tablespoon water	2 tablespoons mixed with 2 tablespoons water
European-style cocoa	⅓ cup	⅔ cup
Puréed dark sweet cherries	½ cup	1 cup
CRUST		
Graham Cracker (page 8)	single recipe	double recipe

Chilling time	2 hours	2 hours
Serves	8	16
Calories per serving	186 (14 from fat)	186 (14 from fat)
Fat per serving	1.6 grams	1.6 grams

No-bake layers of chocolate and cherries make a quick and easy summer dessert.

---

1. Gently pat the prepared crust mixture on the bottom and sides of an 8-inch pie plate (or plates).

2. Blend together the cream cheese and sugar with an electric mixer. Add the whipped topping, yogurt, sour cream, vanilla, and lemon juice. Continue to blend until smooth and well-combined.

3. Drizzle the gelatin over the mixture and fold in gently.

4. Divide the batter in half. Fold the cocoa into one half, and the cherries into the other.

5. Pour the cocoa batter into the prepared crust (or crusts) and smooth with a spatula. Gently spoon the cherry batter on top.

6. Cover with plastic wrap and refrigerate at least 2 hours.

7. Cut into wedges and serve.

No-Bake Orange and Chocolate Cheesecake

INGREDIENT	ONE 8-INCH CAKE	TWO 8-INCH CAKES
Fat-free cream cheese, softened	2 8-ounce packages	4 8-ounce packages
Sugar	¾ cup	1 ½ cups
Low-fat whipped topping	½ cup	1 cup
Fat-free yogurt	¼ cup	½ cup
Fat-free sour cream	¼ cup	½ cup
Vanilla extract	1 teaspoon	2 teaspoons
Fresh lemon juice	½ teaspoon	1 teaspoon
Unflavored gelatin	1 tablespoon mixed with 1 tablespoon water	2 tablespoons mixed with 2 tablespoons water
European-style cocoa	⅓ cup	⅔ cup
Orange juice concentrate	½ cup	1 cup
CRUST		
Zesty Orange Graham Cracker (page 12)	single recipe	double recipe

Chilling time	2 hours	2 hours
Serves	8	16
Calories per serving	187 (14 from fat)	187 (14 from fat)
Fat per serving	1.6 grams	1.6 grams

This popular flavor combination is one of my favorites.

---

1. Gently pat the prepared crust mixture on the bottom and sides of an 8-inch pie plate (or plates).

2. Blend together the cream cheese and sugar with an electric mixer. Add the whipped topping, yogurt, sour cream, vanilla, and lemon juice. Continue to blend until smooth and well-combined.

3. Drizzle the gelatin over the mixture and fold in gently.

4. Divide the batter in half. Fold the cocoa into one half, and the orange juice into the other.

5. Pour the cocoa batter into the prepared crust (or crusts) and smooth with a spatula. Gently spoon the orange batter on top.

6. Cover with plastic wrap and refrigerate at least 2 hours.

7. Cut into wedges and serve.

No-Bake Layered Sensations

No-Bake Chocolate Hazelnut Cheesecake

INGREDIENT	ONE 8-INCH CAKE	TWO 8-INCH CAKES
Fat-free cream cheese, softened	2 8-ounce packages	4 8-ounce packages
Sugar	¾ cup	1½ cups
Low-fat whipped topping	½ cup	1 cup
Fat-free yogurt	¼ cup	½ cup
Fat-free sour cream	¼ cup	½ cup
Vanilla extract	1 teaspoon	2 teaspoons
Fresh lemon juice	½ teaspoon	1 teaspoon
Unflavored gelatin	1 tablespoon mixed with 1 tablespoon water	2 tablespoons mixed with 2 tablespoons water
European-style cocoa	⅓ cup	⅔ cup
Hazelnut extract	2 teaspoons	4 teaspoons
CRUST		
Graham Cracker (page 8)	single recipe	double recipe

Chilling time	2 hours	2 hours
Serves	8	16
Calories per serving	180 (14 from fat)	180 (14 from fat)
Fat per serving	1.6 grams	1.6 grams

Top: Chocolate Raspberry Cheesecake
(page 90)

Bottom Right: Crème de Menthe Cheesecake
(page 116)

Bottom Left: Rose Petal Cheesecake
(page 140)

Top: Marble Swirl Cheesecake (page 78)

Bottom Left: No-Bake Black-and-White
Cheesecake (page 230)

Bottom Right: Orange Creamsicle
Cheesecake (page 186)

As an added touch, garnish this special cake with some chocolate-dipped hazelnuts (page 114).

---

1. Gently pat the prepared crust mixture on the bottom and sides of an 8-inch pie plate (or plates).

2. Blend together the cream cheese and sugar with an electric mixer. Add the whipped topping, yogurt, sour cream, vanilla, and lemon juice. Continue to blend until smooth and well-combined.

3. Drizzle the gelatin over the mixture and fold in gently.

4. Divide the batter in half. Fold the cocoa into one half, and the hazelnut extract into the other.

5. Pour the cocoa batter into the prepared crust (or crusts) and smooth with a spatula. Gently spoon the hazelnut batter on top.

6. Cover with plastic wrap and refrigerate at least 2 hours.

7. Cut into wedges and serve.

No-Bake Peanut Butter Cup Cheesecake

INGREDIENT	ONE 8-INCH CAKE	TWO 8-INCH CAKES
Fat-free cream cheese, softened	2 8-ounce packages	4 8-ounce packages
Sugar	¾ cup	1½ cups
Low-fat whipped topping	½ cup	1 cup
Fat-free yogurt	¼ cup	½ cup
Fat-free sour cream	¼ cup	½ cup
Vanilla extract	1 teaspoon	2 teaspoons
Fresh lemon juice	½ teaspoon	1 teaspoon
Unflavored gelatin	1 tablespoon mixed with 1 tablespoon water	2 tablespoons mixed with 2 tablespoons water
European-style cocoa	¼ cup	½ cup
Reduced-fat peanut butter	⅓ cup	⅔ cup
CRUST		
Chocolate Graham Cracker (page 10)	single recipe	double recipe

Chilling time	2 hours	2 hours
Serves	8	16
Calories per serving	227 (41 from fat)	227 (41 from fat)
Fat per serving	4.6 grams	4.6 grams

When you're in the mood to splurge, try this cheesecake, which is slightly higher in fat than the others.

---

1. Gently pat the prepared crust mixture on the bottom and sides of an 8-inch pie plate (or plates).

2. Blend together the cream cheese and sugar with an electric mixer. Add the whipped topping, yogurt, sour cream, vanilla, and lemon juice. Continue to blend until smooth and well-combined.

3. Drizzle the gelatin over the mixture and fold in gently.

4. Divide the batter in half. Fold the cocoa into one half, and the peanut butter into the other.

5. Pour the cocoa batter into the prepared crust (or crusts) and smooth with a spatula. Gently spoon the peanut butter batter on top.

6. Cover with plastic wrap and refrigerate at least 2 hours.

7. Cut into wedges and serve.

No-Bake Strawberries and Cream Cheesecake

INGREDIENT	ONE 8-INCH CAKE	TWO 8-INCH CAKES
Firm tofu, mashed	1 cup	2 cups
Tahini*	½ cup	1 cup
Chick peas, mashed	½ cup	1 cup
Sugar	¾ cup	1½ cups
Soy milk	½ cup	1 cup
Fresh lemon juice	1 tablespoon	2 tablespoons
Vanilla extract	1 teaspoon	2 teaspoons
Unflavored gelatin	1 tablespoon mixed with 1 tablespoon water	2 tablespoons mixed with 2 tablespoons water
Puréed strawberries, fresh or frozen**	½ cup	1 cup

CRUST		
Graham Cracker (page 8)	single recipe	double recipe

* Tahini (puréed sesame seeds) is available in most supermarkets.
** Be sure to thaw and drain if using frozen variety.

Chilling time	2 hours	2 hours
Serves	8	16
Calories per serving	173 (43 from fat)	173 (43 from fat)
Fat per serving	4.75 grams	4.75 grams

Light and luscious and lactose-free!

---

1. Gently pat the prepared crust mixture on the bottom and sides of an 8-inch pie plate (or plates).

2. Blend together the tofu, tahini, chick peas, and sugar in a food processor. Add the soy milk, lemon juice, and vanilla. Continue to blend until smooth and well-combined.

3. Drizzle the gelatin over the mixture and fold in gently.

4. Divide the batter in half. Fold the strawberries into one half, and leave the other half plain.

5. Pour the strawberry batter into the prepared crust (or crusts) and smooth with a spatula. Gently spoon the plain batter on top.

6. Cover with plastic wrap and refrigerate at least 2 hours.

7. Cut into wedges and serve.

Variations

Instead of strawberries, you can use puréed seedless raspberries, blackberries, or a mixture of your favorite berries.

No-Bake Root Beer Float Cheesecake

INGREDIENT	ONE 8-INCH CAKE	TWO 8-INCH CAKES
Fat-free cream cheese, softened	2 8-ounce packages	4 8-ounce packages
Sugar	¾ cup	1½ cups
Low-fat whipped topping	½ cup	1 cup
Fat-free yogurt	¼ cup	½ cup
Fat-free sour cream	¼ cup	½ cup
Vanilla extract	1 teaspoon	2 teaspoons
Fresh lemon juice	½ teaspoon	1 teaspoon
Unflavored gelatin	1 tablespoon mixed with 1 tablespoon water	2 tablespoons mixed with 2 tablespoons water
2 teaspoons root beer extract	2 teaspoons	4 teaspoons
Mini root beer jelly beans	¼ cup	½ cup

CRUST

Graham Cracker (page 8)	single recipe	double recipe

Chilling Time	2 hours	2 hours
Serves	8	16
Calories per serving	199 (14 from fat)	199 (14 from fat)
Fat per serving	1.6 grams	1.6 grams

You don't have to go to an ice cream parlor to enjoy a rich, creamy root beer float.

---

1. Gently pat the prepared crust mixture on the bottom and sides of an 8-inch pie plate (or plates).

2. Blend together the cream cheese and sugar with an electric mixer. Add the whipped topping, yogurt, sour cream, vanilla, and lemon juice. Continue to blend until smooth and well-combined.

3. Drizzle the gelatin over the mixture and fold in gently.

4. Divide the batter in half. Fold the root beer extract and jelly beans into one half, and leave the other half plain.

5. Pour the root beer batter into the prepared crust (or crusts) and smooth with a spatula. Gently spoon the plain batter on top.

6. Cover with plastic wrap and refrigerate at least 2 hours.

7. Cut into wedges and serve.

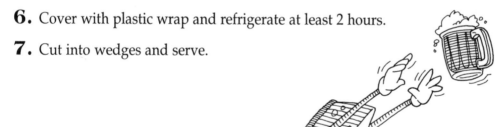

No-Bake Butterscotch and Cream Cheesecake

INGREDIENT	ONE 8-INCH CAKE	TWO 8-INCH CAKES
Fat-free cream cheese, softened	2 8-ounce packages	4 8-ounce packages
Sugar	¾ cup	1½ cups
Low-fat whipped topping	½ cup	1 cup
Fat-free yogurt	¼ cup	½ cup
Fat-free sour cream	¼ cup	½ cup
Vanilla extract	1 teaspoon	2 teaspoons
Fresh lemon juice	½ teaspoon	1 teaspoon
Unflavored gelatin	1 tablespoon mixed with 1 tablespoon water	2 tablespoons mixed with 2 tablespoons water
Fat-free butterscotch ice cream topping	¼ cup	½ cup

CRUST

Graham Cracker (page 8)	single recipe	double recipe

Chilling time	2 hours	2 hours
Serves	8	16
Calories per serving	198 (9 from fat)	198 (9 from fat)
Fat per serving	1 gram	1 gram

Sprinkle with a few crushed butterscotch candies before serving.

---

1. Gently pat the prepared crust mixture on the bottom and sides of an 8-inch pie plate (or plates).

2. Blend together the cream cheese and sugar with an electric mixer. Add the whipped topping, yogurt, sour cream, vanilla, and lemon juice. Continue to blend until smooth and well-combined.

3. Drizzle the gelatin over the mixture and fold in gently.

4. Divide the batter in half. Fold the butterscotch into one half, and leave the other half plain.

5. Pour the butterscotch batter into the prepared crust (or crusts) and smooth with a spatula. Gently spoon the plain batter on top.

6. Cover with plastic wrap and refrigerate at least 2 hours.

7. Cut into wedges and serve.

Variations
You can substitute the butterscotch with any number of fat-free ice cream toppings. Caramel and maple are good choices.

No-Bake Orange Creamsicle Cheesecake

INGREDIENT	ONE 8-INCH CAKE	TWO 8-INCH CAKES
Fat-free cream cheese, softened	2 8-ounce packages	4 8-ounce packages
Sugar	¾ cup	1½ cups
Low-fat whipped topping	½ cup	1 cup
Fat-free yogurt	¼ cup	½ cup
Fat-free sour cream	¼ cup	½ cup
Vanilla extract	1 teaspoon	2 teaspoons
Fresh lemon juice	½ teaspoon	1 teaspoon
Unflavored gelatin	1 tablespoon mixed with 1 tablespoon water	2 tablespoons mixed with 2 tablespoons water
Orange juice concentrate	¼ cup	½ cup

CRUST

Zesty Orange Graham Cracker (page 12)	single recipe	double recipe

Chilling time	2 hours	2 hours
Serves	8	16
Calories per serving	159 (14 from fat)	159 (14 from fat)
Fat per serving	1.6 grams	1.6 grams

This cheesecake is cool, luscious, and delicately sweet.

---

1. Gently pat the prepared crust mixture on the bottom and sides of an 8-inch pie plate (or plates).

2. Blend together the cream cheese and sugar with an electric mixer. Add the whipped topping, yogurt, sour cream, vanilla, and lemon juice. Continue to blend until smooth and well-combined.

3. Drizzle the gelatin over the mixture and fold in gently.

4. Divide the batter in half. Fold the orange juice into one half, and leave the other half plain.

5. Pour the orange batter into the prepared crust (or crusts) and smooth with a spatula. Gently spoon the plain batter on top.

6. Cover with plastic wrap and refrigerate at least 2 hours.

7. Cut into wedges and serve.

Variation

For a grape creamsicle cheesecake, use purple grape juice concentrate instead of orange.

No-Bake Watermelon and Cream Cheesecake

INGREDIENT	ONE 8-INCH CAKE	TWO 8-INCH CAKES
Fat-free cream cheese, softened	2 8-ounce packages	4 8-ounce packages
Sugar	¾ cup	1½ cups
Low-fat whipped topping	½ cup	1 cup
Fat-free yogurt	¼ cup	½ cup
Fat-free sour cream	¼ cup	½ cup
Vanilla extract	1 teaspoon	2 teaspoons
Fresh lemon juice	½ teaspoon	1 teaspoon
Unflavored gelatin	1 tablespoon mixed with 1 tablespoon water	2 tablespoons mixed with 2 tablespoons water
Puréed watermelon, well-drained	¼ cup	½ cup
CRUST		
Graham Cracker (page 8)	single recipe	double recipe

Chilling time	2 hours	2 hours
Serves	8	16
Calories per serving	146 (9 from fat)	146 (9 from fat)
Fat per serving	1 gram	1 gram

Be sure the watermelon is well-drained before adding it to the batter.

---

1. Gently pat the prepared crust mixture on the bottom and sides of an 8-inch pie plate (or plates).

2. Blend together the cream cheese and sugar with an electric mixer. Add the whipped topping, yogurt, sour cream, vanilla, and lemon juice. Continue to blend until smooth and well-combined.

3. Drizzle the gelatin over the mixture and fold in gently.

4. Divide the batter in half. Fold the watermelon into one half, and leave the other half plain.

5. Pour the watermelon batter into the prepared crust (or crusts) and smooth with a spatula. Gently spoon the plain batter on top.

6. Cover with plastic wrap and refrigerate at least 2 hours.

7. Cut into wedges and serve.

Variations

Puréed mango and honeydew are other good fruits to use with this recipe. Or try a combination of your favorite melons.

No-Bake Pineapple with Coconut Cream Cheesecake

INGREDIENT	ONE 8-INCH CAKE	TWO 8-INCH CAKES
Fat-free cream cheese, softened	2 8-ounce packages	4 8-ounce packages
Sugar	¾ cup	1½ cups
Low-fat whipped topping	½ cup	1 cup
Fat-free yogurt	¼ cup	½ cup
Fat-free sour cream	¼ cup	½ cup
Vanilla extract	1 teaspoon	2 teaspoons
Fresh lemon juice	½ teaspoon	1 teaspoon
Unflavored gelatin	1 tablespoon mixed with 1 tablespoon water	2 tablespoons mixed with 2 tablespoons water
Crushed pineapple, drained	¼ cup	½ cup
Coconut extract	1 teaspoon	2 teaspoons
CRUST		
Coconut Oat (page 32)	single recipe	double recipe

Chilling time	2 hours	2 hours
Serves	8	16
Calories per serving	152 (9 from fat)	152 (9 from fat)
Fat per serving	1 gram	1 gram

Refreshingly tropical, this cheesecake is a superb summertime treat.

---

1. Gently pat the prepared crust mixture on the bottom and sides of an 8-inch pie plate (or plates).

2. Blend together the cream cheese and sugar with an electric mixer. Add the whipped topping, yogurt, sour cream, vanilla, and lemon juice. Continue to blend until smooth and well-combined.

3. Drizzle the gelatin over the mixture and fold in gently.

4. Divide the batter in half. Fold the pineapple into one half, and the coconut extract into the other.

5. Pour the pineapple batter into the prepared crust (or crusts) and smooth with a spatula. Gently spoon the coconut batter on top.

6. Cover with plastic wrap and refrigerate at least 2 hours.

7. Cut into wedges and serve.

No-Bake Amaretto and Cream Cheesecake

INGREDIENT	ONE 8-INCH CAKE	TWO 8-INCH CAKES
Fat-free cream cheese, softened	2 8-ounce packages	4 8-ounce packages
Sugar	¾ cup	1½ cups
Low-fat whipped topping	½ cup	1 cup
Fat-free yogurt	¼ cup	½ cup
Fat-free sour cream	¼ cup	½ cup
Vanilla extract	1 teaspoon	2 teaspoons
Fresh lemon juice	½ teaspoon	1 teaspoon
Unflavored gelatin	1 tablespoon mixed with 1 tablespoon water	2 tablespoons mixed with 2 tablespoons water
Amaretto liqueur	¼ cup	½ cup
CRUST		
Graham Cracker (page 8)	single recipe	double recipe

Chilling time	2 hours	2 hours
Serves	8	16
Calories per serving	223 (14 from fat)	223 (14 from fat)
Fat per serving	1.6 grams	1.6 grams

This creamy cheesecake is packed with almond flavor.

---

1. Gently pat the prepared crust mixture on the bottom and sides of an 8-inch pie plate (or plates).

2. Blend together the cream cheese and sugar with an electric mixer. Add the whipped topping, yogurt, sour cream, vanilla, and lemon juice. Continue to blend until smooth and well-combined.

3. Drizzle the gelatin over the mixture and fold in gently.

4. Divide the batter in half. Fold the amaretto into one half, and leave the other half plain.

5. Pour the amaretto batter into the prepared crust (or crusts) and smooth with a spatula. Gently spoon the plain batter on top.

6. Cover with plastic wrap and refrigerate at least 2 hours.

7. Cut into wedges and serve.

No-Bake Roses and Cream Cheesecake

INGREDIENT	ONE 8-INCH CAKE	TWO 8-INCH CAKES
Fat-free cream cheese, softened	2 8-ounce packages	4 8-ounce packages
Sugar	¾ cup	1½ cups
Low-fat whipped topping	½ cup	1 cup
Fat-free yogurt	¼ cup	½ cup
Fat-free sour cream	¼ cup	½ cup
Vanilla extract	1 teaspoon	2 teaspoons
Fresh lemon juice	½ teaspoon	1 teaspoon
Unflavored gelatin	1 tablespoon mixed with 1 tablespoon water	2 tablespoons mixed with 2 tablespoons water
Rose syrup*	¼ cup	½ cup
Red food coloring	2 drops	4 drops
CRUST		
Graham Cracker (page 8)	single recipe	double recipe

* Rose syrup is available in Greek and Middle Eastern markets. To make your own, see recipe on page 154.

Chilling time	2 hours	2 hours
Serves	8	16
Calories per serving	189 (9 from fat)	189 (9 from fat)
Fat per serving	1 gram	1 gram

Delicately flavored and delicious.

---

1. Gently pat the prepared crust mixture on the bottom and sides of an 8-inch pie plate (or plates).

2. Blend together the cream cheese and sugar with an electric mixer. Add the whipped topping, yogurt, sour cream, vanilla, and lemon juice. Continue to blend until smooth and well-combined.

3. Drizzle the gelatin over the mixture and fold in gently.

4. Divide the batter in half. Fold the rose syrup and food coloring into one half, and leave the other half plain.

5. Pour the rose batter into the prepared crust (or crusts) and smooth with a spatula. Gently spoon the plain batter on top.

6. Cover with plastic wrap and refrigerate at least 2 hours.

7. Cut into wedges and serve.

No-Bake Café au Lait Cheesecake

INGREDIENT	ONE 8-INCH CAKE	TWO 8-INCH CAKES
Fat-free cream cheese, softened	2 8-ounce packages	4 8-ounce packages
Sugar	¾ cup	1½ cups
Low-fat whipped topping	½ cup	1 cup
Fat-free yogurt	¼ cup	½ cup
Fat-free sour cream	¼ cup	½ cup
Vanilla extract	1 teaspoon	2 teaspoons
Fresh lemon juice	½ teaspoon	1 teaspoon
Unflavored gelatin	1 tablespoon mixed with 1 tablespoon water	2 tablespoons mixed with 2 tablespoons water
Instant coffee granules	2 teaspoons	4 teaspoons

CRUST

Graham Cracker (page 8)	single recipe	double recipe

Chilling time	2 hours	2 hours
Serves	8	16
Calories per serving	171 (9 from fat)	171 (9 from fat)
Fat per serving	1 gram	1 gram

You can add a few coffee-flavored jelly beans to the coffee layer of this cheesecake.

---

1. Gently pat the prepared crust mixture on the bottom and sides of an 8-inch pie plate (or plates).

2. Blend together the cream cheese and sugar with an electric mixer. Add the whipped topping, yogurt, sour cream, vanilla, and lemon juice. Continue to blend until smooth and well-combined.

3. Drizzle the gelatin over the mixture and fold in gently.

4. Divide the batter in half. Fold the coffee granules into one half, and leave the other half plain.

5. Pour the coffee batter into the prepared crust (or crusts) and smooth with a spatula. Gently spoon the plain batter on top.

6. Cover with plastic wrap and refrigerate at least 2 hours.

7. Cut into wedges and serve.

No-Bake Pumpkin and Cream Cheesecake

INGREDIENT	ONE 8-INCH CAKE	TWO 8-INCH CAKES
Fat-free cream cheese, softened	2 8-ounce packages	4 8-ounce packages
Sugar	¾ cup	1½ cups
Low-fat whipped topping	½ cup	1 cup
Fat-free yogurt	¼ cup	½ cup
Fat-free sour cream	¼ cup	½ cup
Vanilla extract	1 teaspoon	2 teaspoons
Fresh lemon juice	½ teaspoon	1 teaspoon
Unflavored gelatin	1 tablespoon mixed with 1 tablespoon water	2 tablespoons mixed with 2 tablespoons water
Canned pumpkin	⅓ cup	⅔ cup
Pumpkin pie spice	1 teaspoon	2 teaspoons

CRUST

Cinnamon Graham Cracker (page 18)	single recipe	double recipe

Chilling time	2 hours	2 hours
Serves	8	16
Calories per serving	176 (9 from fat)	176 (9 from fat)
Fat per serving	1 gram	1 gram

An excellent choice for your holiday table.

1. Gently pat the prepared crust mixture on the bottom and sides of an 8-inch pie plate (or plates).

2. Blend together the cream cheese and sugar with an electric mixer. Add the whipped topping, yogurt, sour cream, vanilla, and lemon juice. Continue to blend until smooth and well-combined.

3. Drizzle the gelatin over the mixture and fold in gently.

4. Divide the batter in half. Fold the pumpkin and pumpkin pie spice into one half, and leave the other half plain.

5. Pour the pumpkin batter into the prepared crust (or crusts) and smooth with a spatula. Gently spoon the plain batter on top.

6. Cover with plastic wrap and refrigerate at least 2 hours.

7. Cut into wedges and serve.

No-Bake Layered Sensations

No-Bake Lemon and Cream Cheesecake

INGREDIENT	ONE 8-INCH CAKE	TWO 8-INCH CAKES
Fat-free cream cheese, softened	2 8-ounce packages	4 8-ounce packages
Sugar	¾ cup	1½ cups
Low-fat whipped topping	½ cup	1 cup
Fat-free yogurt	¼ cup	½ cup
Fat-free sour cream	¼ cup	½ cup
Vanilla extract	1 teaspoon	2 teaspoons
Unflavored gelatin	1 tablespoon mixed with 1 tablespoon water	2 tablespoons mixed with 2 tablespoons water
Fresh lemon juice	⅓ cup	⅔ cup
Yellow food coloring	2 drops	4 drops
CRUST		
Lemony Graham Cracker (page 14)	single recipe	double recipe

Chilling time	2 hours	2 hours
Serves	8	16
Calories per serving	183 (14 from fat)	183 (14 from fat)
Fat per serving	1.6 grams	1.6 grams

These rich, creamy layers are the perfect ending to a light summer meal.

---

1. Gently pat the prepared crust mixture on the bottom and sides of an 8-inch pie plate (or plates).

2. Blend together the cream cheese and sugar with an electric mixer. Add the whipped topping, yogurt, sour cream, and vanilla. Continue to blend until smooth and well-combined.

3. Drizzle the gelatin over the mixture and fold in gently.

4. Divide the batter in half. Fold the lemon juice and food coloring into one half, and leave the other half plain.

5. Pour the lemon batter into the prepared crust (or crusts) and smooth with a spatula. Gently spoon the plain batter on top.

6. Cover with plastic wrap and refrigerate at least 2 hours.

7. Cut into wedges and serve.

No-Bake Lime and Cream Cheesecake

INGREDIENT	ONE 8-INCH CAKE	TWO 8-INCH CAKES
Fat-free cream cheese, softened	2 8-ounce packages	4 8-ounce packages
Sugar	¾ cup	1½ cups
Low-fat whipped topping	½ cup	1 cup
Fat-free yogurt	¼ cup	½ cup
Fat-free sour cream	¼ cup	½ cup
Vanilla extract	1 teaspoon	2 teaspoons
Unflavored gelatin	1 tablespoon mixed with 1 tablespoon water	2 tablespoons mixed with 2 tablespoons water
Lime juice	⅓ cup	⅔ cup
Green food coloring	2 drops	4 drops
CRUST		
Zesty Lime Oat (page 28)	single recipe	double recipe

Chilling time	2 hours	2 hours
Serves	8	16
Calories per serving	183 (14 from fat)	183 (14 from fat)
Fat per serving	1.6 grams	1.6 grams

The lime flavor comes through loud and clear in this lovely layered cheesecake.

1. Gently pat the prepared crust mixture on the bottom and sides of an 8-inch pie plate (or plates).

2. Blend together the cream cheese and sugar with an electric mixer. Add the whipped topping, yogurt, sour cream, and vanilla. Continue to blend until smooth and well-combined.

3. Drizzle the gelatin over the mixture and fold in gently.

4. Divide the batter in half. Fold the lime juice and food coloring into one half, and leave the other half plain.

5. Pour the lime batter into the prepared crust (or crusts) and smooth with a spatula. Gently spoon the plain batter on top.

6. Cover with plastic wrap and refrigerate at least 2 hours.

7. Cut into wedges and serve.

No-Bake Lemon-Lime Cheesecake

INGREDIENT	ONE 8-INCH CAKE	TWO 8-INCH CAKES
Fat-free cream cheese, softened	2 8-ounce packages	4 8-ounce packages
Sugar	¾ cup	1½ cups
Low-fat whipped topping	½ cup	1 cup
Fat-free yogurt	¼ cup	½ cup
Fat-free sour cream	¼ cup	½ cup
Vanilla extract	1 teaspoon	2 teaspoons
Unflavored gelatin	1 tablespoon mixed with 1 tablespoon water	2 tablespoons mixed with 2 tablespoons water
Fresh lemon juice	2 ½ tablespoons	5 tablespoons
Lime juice	2 ½ tablespoons	5 tablespoons
Yellow food coloring	2 drops	4 drops
Green food coloring	2 drops	4 drops

CRUST

Lemony Graham Cracker (page 14)	single recipe	double recipe

Chilling time	2 hours	2 hours
Serves	8	16
Calories per serving	183 (14 from fat)	183 (14 from fat)
Fat per serving	1.6 grams	1.6 grams

If you love citrus, this is the cheesecake for you.

1. Gently pat the prepared crust mixture on the bottom and sides of an 8-inch pie plate (or plates).

2. Blend together the cream cheese and sugar with an electric mixer. Add the whipped topping, yogurt, sour cream, and vanilla. Continue to blend until smooth and well-combined.

3. Drizzle the gelatin over the mixture and fold in gently.

4. Divide the batter in half. Stir the lemon juice and yellow food coloring into one half, and the lime juice and green food coloring into the other.

5. Pour the lime batter into the prepared crust (or crusts) and smooth with a spatula. Gently spoon the lemon batter on top.

6. Cover with plastic wrap and refrigerate at least 2 hours.

7. Cut into wedges and serve.

Index

311